On Eagle's Wings

*A mother's story of hope and healing
amidst suffering and loss*

Diana Stroh

On Eagle's Wings
A mother's story of hope and healing amidst suffering and loss

Printed in the United States of America

ISBN: 1450567932
EAN: 9781450567930

I dedicate this book to my firstborn son, Derrick Edward Cotterman. You were the first to teach me about unconditional and selfless love. What you taught me in life you taught me through death. You remain forever in my heart and I long for the day when we will be reunited.

Acknowledgements

With special gratitude to—

My husband Carl,

 God hand-picked you to walk alongside me through this journey of healing. I am so honored that I could share my joys and sorrows with you. I could not have asked for a better partner.

My son Travis,

 You are an inspiration to the power and grace of God's love. You should have never had to experience such pain and sorrow at such a tender age. May you never forget how much God loves you.

My son and daughter, Christopher and Erika,

 You ache in your hearts for a brother you never knew. I have spoken much about your big brother in heaven. May this book give you a glimpse of what he was like. More importantly, may you long for your eternal home as much as I do.

My parents, Dieter and Hilde, and my sisters, Rosi and Monica,

 How incredibly difficult it must have been for you to hear of the sudden news of Derrick's death. What a huge burden you carried living so far away and not being able to love and support me in person. Thank you for being my prayer warriors who stormed the throne room of God on my behalf. May you know that your prayers were not only heard, but also answered.

And most of all,
My Heavenly Father,

Thank you for the vision you put in my heart to write this book. You, above all, know how incredibly difficult it was at times to write it. You have placed in my heart a passion to pass on my story of healing. You drastically altered my life and gave me renewed hope and strength. May my story resonate of your love, mercy, and grace, and may the afflicted hear what you have done in my life and rejoice, knowing that you can do the same for them. May this book only bring glory to you and healing to many sons and daughters.

Table of Contents

A Personal Note from the Author

This book has been a long time coming. I have known for quite some time that I need to write it. I have a story worth telling. But then again, so do you. Each one of us has a story that needs to be retold—a legacy that needs to be left behind when we are no longer here. I have held off writing this book because in order to do so, I must go back in time. Back to darker days filled with anguish and pain. By the power of God's amazing grace, I have moved on to better days. So I had to ask myself, "Why would I want to go back in time to relive painful memories?" Don't get me wrong—going back also brings floods of wonderful treasured memories. Memories that deserve retelling. Memories of my beautiful firstborn son who taught me so much about life. However, accompanying these happy memories are sorrowful ones too. My son not only taught me about life, he also taught me about death.

Then God gave me the dream—the dream that said it was time to tell my story. You see, it really is not about me at all. It is about God and his life-saving, transforming power at work in all of us who believe. Believe that there are better tomorrows. That there really is purpose in pain and suffering. That He has a purpose and a plan for each one of us. And that it really is all about Him. That is why I am writing this book. My prayer is that everyone who reads it, will find new purpose and meaning for his life and come to recognize that with God all things are possible. May I be a walking testimony of His love and may He receive all the glory that is due Him. I am just the vessel He is using to tell a poignant story about His great love, mercy, and grace.

Prologue

On February 10, 1990, the world as I knew it came to an end. At least for me it did. That day will be forever etched in my mind as it marked the end of a glorious dream. I was thrust into a fiery battlefield—a place where I did not want to be. My firstborn 9 year old son died on that somber day and now a battle was waging for my soul. As I entered into unknown territory, I began the roller coaster ride of my life. I never knew such extreme emotions existed. How could I possibly go on without my son? As days turned into weeks and weeks turned into months, I finally faced my 'crisis hour' fully recognizing my own inadequacy to handle what lie ahead. It was then that I finally surrendered all. I surrendered my hopes and dreams. I surrendered my own wisdom and strength. And ultimately, I surrendered my son, Derrick, to God.

I cast myself hopelessly at His feet. Somehow I knew there was no way out of this hard and narrow place but at the top. God himself rescued me from the pit of darkness and despair, but my deliverance came by rising higher and coming into a new experience with Him. In His love and mercy, Jesus carried me on eagle's wings and brought me to Himself (Exodus 19:4).

God's Spirit lifted me to new heights, above the wind, above the rain, above the earth, and mostly, above my agonizing circumstances. As I placed my hope in Jesus Christ alone, resting and believing in the promises of His Word, His strength enabled me to rise above my life's confusing and bitter difficulties. As I trusted Him, I expectantly and patiently waited for deliverance.

"He turned to me and heard my cry. He lifted me out of the slimy pit, out of the mud and mire; he set my feet on a rock and gave me a firm place to stand. He put a new song in my mouth, a hymn of praise to our God. Many will see and fear and put their trust in the Lord." Psalm 40:1-3

My heart is filled with gratitude to God, my Father, my Redeemer, and my Deliverer. Because of His endless supply of grace and goodness which He lavishly bestowed upon me, I can sing once again. He has put a rainbow in the sky which reminds me of all of His precious promises. His truth has set me free indeed, and together we are now soaring on the wings of eagles.

"But those who hope in the Lord will renew their strength. They will soar on wings like eagles; they will run and not grow weary, they will walk and not be faint." Isaiah 40:31

THE DREAM   1

"In the last days," God says, "I will pour out my Spirit on all people. Your sons and daughters will prophesy, your young men will see visions, your old men will dream dreams."

Acts 2:17

I used to wonder if God still spoke to us through dreams. I know He often communicated His will to people through dreams during the Old Testament times. After personally experiencing it myself, I can now positively affirm that I *know* He still speaks through dreams. The God of the universe can communicate with us any way He chooses, and sometimes He chooses to speak directly to the deepest places in our hearts through our subconscious mind. Maybe He chooses to reveal Himself to us in that way because we could not handle what He would have to say otherwise. Or maybe we are just too busy to hear His soft, still voice. Sometimes He graciously gives us glimpses of heaven and of our loved ones through these vividly intense dreams.

Although I have not had many dreams that came directly from heaven's throne, the few that I have had the privilege of experiencing have remained with me forever. Without a shadow of a doubt, these dreams were direct communications from God himself. The book you are now reading has come to fruition because of one such dream. Many years earlier, God's voice whispered to my spirit to document my story, and then 6-1/2 years later my dream confirmed that it was time to begin.

It was November 9, 2007, a day that I will long remember. This is the day that I received a special surprise visit from my son, Derrick. Of course, not in a tangible way, but deep in my subconscious, in a place where I was fully present neither on earth nor in heaven. Derrick visited me in my dreams. I had known since May of 2001 that I was to write a book about Derrick and what his death had taught me about God, myself, and life. Over the years many people have also encouraged me to document my story because it inspired them in some way.

I was actively seeking God for His timing regarding the writing of this book. I had just finished a 22-month college program to earn my Bachelor of Science degree and was now working part-time as a preschool teacher at our church. It seemed as if there was always something to do and yet never enough time. Even though a part of me really wanted to begin writing, I was not quite sure how to begin, so I began praying to God and asking Him to give me some clear indication when to start on this immense project. I knew it would require God's involvement for I could never do such a monumental task in my own strength.

Back to my dream—During the morning hours, while the entire house was still asleep, I awoke to the sound of a ringing doorbell. I soon became aware that I was the only one who could hear it. Sluggish from being abruptly awoken, it took me several minutes to climb out of bed. My feet finally hit the floor and I descended the stairs to investigate who could be at my door so early in the morning. To my dismay, when I reached the door and opened it no one was there. Maybe someone was playing a prank. It was still very dark outside, and I slowly turned my head from right to left, but still saw no one. My eyes finally focused straight ahead toward the front yard when I noticed the darkness begin to fade. Suddenly it became quite bright and a dark-stained wooden picnic table in the middle of the front yard came to my view. Derrick was sitting on the bench facing the house and he was deeply immersed in reading. When he became aware of my presence, he lowered the book and gave me a big smile and a wave. I could not believe that it was him, so I called out his name—"Derrick." Instantly he was transported onto my lap, and I was now sitting on the front porch steps cradling him. He was just as I had remembered—a young 9 year old boy. I began to lightly stroke his cheek as I repeatedly said, "Derrick, I love you. Derrick, I love you, Derrick, I love you." "I know Mom," was his only reply, and then he was gone and my dream was over. Oh, if he would just come back and stay awhile longer.

I awoke from my dream and realized that I had spent a precious few moments with my boy. I was not hallucinating and it was not just some weird fantasy—it was so very real. The fact that I remembered the dream so intensely the next day, the next month, and the next year, made it all the more real to me. God allowed me an encounter with my son through this vivid dream. The vision of Derrick remained with me day after day, and I intuitively believed that there was some special significance to this dream.

It did not take long to decipher its meaning—at least parts of it. Everyone was asleep and no one heard the doorbell but me. This dream was clearly for my eyes only as I was the one beckoned to the front door. At first it was so dark and I could not see anything or anyone, and then the darkness faded and it became quite bright. When I tried to look through my own eyes I saw only darkness. Since Derrick is not living here in the flesh, he came to me through a bright light. It takes the eyes of faith to see invisible things. When he was instantly transported to my lap and I was able to stroke his cheek provided me with an opportunity to let him know how much I loved him. He left so abruptly that Friday night, and there were no hugs or 'I Love You's.' It was as if God gave me another chance to tell him how much I loved and missed him.

One piece of the puzzle that did not make sense was why Derrick was sitting at the picnic table reading a book. He did love to read and one night as I went to check on him before retiring myself, I found him hiding under the bed covers with a flashlight reading a book. One of his favorite books was *James and the Giant Peach* by Roald Dahl. So maybe this book in my dream was another great children's story.

Not long after I had this special visit from Derrick, I shared my testimony with a friend at my son, Christopher's, basketball game. She had just found out through a mutual friend that I had lost a child to death many years ago. I filled in the missing pieces and explained to her the instrumental role God played in my life in bringing me healing. She listened intently and through teary eyes implored me to write a book. I never thought much about that conversation until the next day. My husband and I were deep in conversation about relationships and how they take time and commitment to truly flourish the way God intends for them to. I previously shared with Carl and my children, Chris and Erika, my very poignant dream. However, I do not know if any of them truly understood how very real this dream was to me.

That night as I was getting ready for bed my mind went back to my previous conversation with my friend. I felt honored that she would even want to read a book about my son. Then out of the clear blue, I heard a voice deep within my spirit speak, "The book Derrick is reading is *YOURS.*" "What? God, is that you?" I could not believe what I just heard. God chose to reveal to me the significance of the dream by allowing all of the pieces of the puzzle to fit together perfectly. I now understood its full meaning.

When Derrick was sitting at the picnic table reading a book, it was **this** book he was reading. The entire dream was God's way of telling me that **now** was the time to begin writing my story. He was challenging and asking me if I would take the time and make the commitment to bring this book to fruition. God knew it would require old wounds to be opened and re-examined. Would I be willing to go back to a very painful period of my life and attempt to capture all of my emotions on paper? God placed an overwhelming desire in my heart to let others know of His abundant love, comfort, and peace. I knew that I must be obedient.

I will never forget the look on my little boy's face as he put down the book for a moment to smile at me. This vision remains etched in my mind. The thought of Derrick reading about his life and how God used it to minister to not only me, but to many others is a story worth retelling. Yes, I would write my story. After all, Derrick is waiting to read it.

Dear Derrick,

I know you have waited a very long time to read this book. How I thank you for visiting me in my dreams and allowing me to hold you once again to tell you how much I love you. Even though your visit was brief, I have cherished and stored the memories of it in my heart. The thought of you reading this book has spurred me on with conviction to write it, no matter what the cost. It did not matter that it would bring back painful memories and tears. Your life, though so brief, was so very precious to me, and it deserves retelling. I want you to know Derrick that you did not die in vain. Do you know how devoted I am to Jesus Christ, my Savior? Do you know that He rescued me from the deepest, darkest pit of despair and brought such joy into my life? Can you feel the love I have for Him in my heart? I know it must only be a fraction of the love you experience in heaven being right there with Him. Though I miss you immensely, it would be so very selfish of me to ask to have you back. I know you are in a much better place and would never want to leave Jesus to return to earth, so please visit me periodically in my dreams. They are so precious to me.

I cannot wait until the day when I will see you again. Jesus has already assured me that you will be the first one in heaven I get to see. I can picture it so vividly in my mind. We will run toward one another and then embrace like never before. Will you still be a child? Will you look the same? Although I am not sure, I think so. Time has no boundaries in heaven and we are sure to recognize one another. Until then, my dear son, I will live out the days God has ordained for me, never losing sight of the reason I am here. I pray that my life will glorify God and that He will be proud of me.

I can almost see your smile as the book has finally made its way into your little hands. Hopefully the pages will allow you to see what an integral part you had in God's shaping my life. I would not be who I am today if it were not for you. God used the pain of losing you to mold me from this big lump of clay into a vessel through which He can pour His living water out of. Yes, the Master Potter is hard at work transforming lives. It is His specialty you know. He may, however, have some more work to do on this one, because I still leak a little now and then. I will see you again when He is satisfied with the result. I know the reunion will be so sweet. Until then, never forget how much I love you.

Love, Your Mom

My Little Angel 2

For you created my inmost being; you knit me together in my mother's womb. I praise you because I am fearfully and wonderfully made; your works are wonderful, I know that full well. My frame was not hidden from you when I was made in the secret place. When I was woven together in the depths of the earth, your eyes saw my unformed body. All the days ordained for me were written in your book before one of them came to be.

Psalm 139:13-16

September 21, 1980, was one of the happiest days of my life. On that day I joined the rank of millions of other women before me who were given the awesome privilege and title of being called, 'Mom.' I was young—precisely twenty years old. But even amidst my immaturity, I instinctively knew that what just happened to me was a magnificent miracle. Out of that enormously round, protruding belly that had been growing larger by the day, burst forth a beautiful baby boy. Of course, I knew all about anatomy and reproduction, but it sure is something different altogether when you personally experience the growth and birth of a child. In fact, I question how anyone can not believe in a supreme and sovereign God after witnessing and experiencing such a miraculous event! Man is truly without excuse, or just plain blind.

He was a rather substantial baby if I do say so myself. Almost nine pounds—8 lbs. 15 oz. to be exact, and 21 inches long! Maybe this was due in part to my being seventeen days past my due date of September 4th. Nonetheless, he was strikingly handsome even for his young age. I could not wait to be alone with him to unwrap the receiving blanket he was swaddled in and study his little frame. Yes, indeed, he was perfectly formed. He looked so robust and healthy compared to the five pound baby my roommate just delivered. I remember laying the two of our babies next to one another to compare their size. Boy, was I glad I got the big one! He was my first, and I was scared enough about how to take care of him let alone worry about how tiny and frail he truly was.

He was born at precisely 12:05 a.m. after only four hours of labor. Thank goodness it was a short labor, because I gave birth to him with no drug assistance. That's right—completely au naturel. That's how I wanted it. Besides it was good to feel a little pain. I did not want to be so drugged up that I missed the whole thing. No, I wanted to remember this event forever.

We named him Derrick. Derrick Edward Cotterman. Edward after his paternal grandfather who died while I was pregnant. And Derrick just because it was different. I liked the name. I never knew any Derrick's. So that was good. I did not want his name to be like anyone else's that I knew. He was given a special name because he was a special child. A child of God. Time would only tell how truly special this little boy was.

I was so excited that I could not get to sleep. For heaven's sake, I just experienced something so incredibly amazing—I gave birth to a real live human being! Furthermore, I was thrilled that he was a boy. I never had any brothers. Two sisters, that's all. I knew my parents would be ecstatic to finally have a boy in the family. The icing on the cake was not only was he my first child, he was also the first grandchild on both sides of the family. Now that was something worth celebrating!

I was so extremely exhilarated that I kept rehearsing the events of the evening over and over in my mind. I decided to write my new baby boy a letter that would be saved until he was older. These were not the days of video cameras rolling to soft music playing in the background as members of the family alternated visits to the delivery room to witness the birth. No, for me it was a very private matter. Just me, his father, the doctor, and a nurse. And God of course. I know He was smiling down on us. He had special plans for this little child. I believe His heart was especially close to my little boy's heart. God knew he did not have much time. But He also knew that Derrick's life would impact many others beyond his years and that time had no boundaries on him.

Dear Derrick,

What an amazing and awesome experience it was giving birth to you. Even though I was so very young, I fully understood the miracle that was transpiring in front of my very own eyes. You were such a beautiful baby, and can I tell you that I was so happy you were a boy! Having grown up with two sisters made it extra special for me to experience the 'boy' thing with you.

I could not wait until the nurse brought you into my room so that I could hold you and study your tiny frame. You looked at me with those big eyes like you knew exactly who I was. I know you recognized my voice because you had heard it for nine months now.

I resigned from my job so that I could be home with you full-time. I innately understood that being a mommy would be a lot of work, and I did not want to miss a thing—your first crawl, first steps, first words. I also hoped you'd be patient with me, because I was sure that I'd make some mistakes along the way. After all, you were my first, and I did not have much experience. Somehow I just knew you would understand.

I loved you so much already and could not wait for our future to unfold together. In the meantime, I would try to be the best mommy ever because you deserved that.

Love, Your Mom

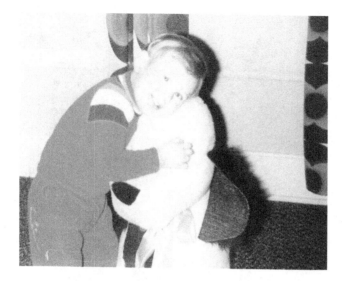

Derrick at 1 year of age.

One of my favorite pictures of Derrick when he was 2-1/2 years old, playing on his swing set.

Derrick after his first pro haircut at 3 years of age.

A Special Connection   3

At that time Jesus said, "I praise you Father, Lord of heaven and earth, because you have hidden these things from the wise and learned, and revealed them to little children. Yes, Father, for this was your good pleasure."   Matthew 11:25

Derrick was an easy baby to care for. Just days after I brought him home from the hospital he slept through the night. He ate well and was generally a very happy baby. I am grateful that he was not a difficult child to raise, because to be brutally honest, I really did not know what I was doing anyway. The only exposure I had to babies was the meager babysitting experience I had during my teenage years.

Many times I think that the firstborn child is sort of a 'guinea pig.' Regardless of your age, you only become proficient at this enormous task through lots and lots of practice, advice, and unfortunately, many mistakes. You simply learn by doing. More often than not, you do things the wrong way. Or at least not like the experts would recommend. But who and what define an expert anyway? What qualities must you possess to be an expert at raising a child? Every single child is not only unique, but also has a different temperament. What works for one child may not work for another. Furthermore, each mom and dad has unique backgrounds they bring to the table as well. Throw that in the mix with the life stage they are in at the time they become parents, and, well—let's just say that all of these greatly impact how they react to and raise their own children.

We were young. Twenty and twenty-two—just kids ourselves, or at the very least very immature adults. Now we were to embark on a whole new adventure being given the biggest responsibility of our entire lives—raising a child. No previous experience, no training, nothing. This little helpless human being would need to not only survive, but also thrive in his new world. What an awesome privilege, yet monumental task God placed before us. Would we be able to not only take care of his needs, but also raise him in a loving home? I was adamant that I would be a great mom. So I resigned from my job as a clerk typist at Ohio Casualty Insurance Company and began the most challenging and fulfilling role of my entire life—motherhood.

What a beautiful little boy Derrick was! Now I know every parent says that about his child, but Derrick was truly a beautiful baby, and he grew into a sweet, sensitive, little boy. White blond hair, fair skin, and bright, big, blue eyes. The kind of eyes that girls love and wish they had! He grew in size so rapidly, and it quickly became apparent to me that he would take after my side of the family. He had my facial features, my blue eyes, and my long legs. My pediatrician calculated when he was two years old that he would be a very tall man one day—6' 3" at least.

I also remember what a bright and intelligent child Derrick was. He grew up so incredibly fast. Not just in size and weight, but in intelligence too. He had quite an extensive vocabulary at a very young age. I read a lot of books to him, and this may explain why he retained so many adult words. He absolutely adored books, especially books about planes, trains, construction trucks, or any other moving vehicles. One of his favorite early phrases was, "That's ridiculous, sure is." I would laugh hysterically when he said that and other funny phrases. He loved receiving positive attention, and he was a little clown from the very beginning.

He did everything early—his first tooth came in at five months, he took his first steps at ten months, he was weaned from the bottle at twelve months, and from the pacifier shortly after that. He did not particularly like naps and often cried when I would put him down for his afternoon nap. But I needed a break, so nap time it was. I am sure he thought he would miss out on something special. I have vivid memories of putting him down for bedtime. He was in a big boy bed before the age of two and would frequently get out of bed. I'd find him lying on the top section of the staircase on the wooden steps, curled up, and sound asleep. Just to be a little closer to us and to hear our voices would suffice. He knew that mommy and daddy would not be pleased if he repeatedly came down to us, so he settled himself on one of the steps and before long fell fast asleep.

When his baby brother, Travis, arrived just two years later, Derrick had to give up his crib, his stroller, and all other baby paraphernalia. Looking back now, what was I thinking? A 2 year old is still a baby in his own right. But I think his extreme intelligence and witty manner made me treat him as if he were much older. Derrick would often speak for Travis which is why I believe Travis did not begin talking nearly as early as Derrick did. Neither did he walk early—he was thirteen months before he took his first steps. But when he did, he would have to be quick to follow his big brother.

Derrick loved his baby brother. I have countless memories of the two of them interacting with each other. From simple things such as banging on bowls with wooden spoons, playing with action figures, and inventing little games, these two little boys were inseparable. They played with each other so well that the term 'sibling rivalry' seemed but a delusion. They especially enjoyed playing 'Batman and Robin' and they would ask me for capes and gloves and various articles of clothing so they would look authentic. Of course, Derrick was always Batman, and Travis was always Robin. They would play this make-believe game for hours at a time. Travis was all too willing to oblige Derrick and would do whatever his big brother wanted. It was a blessing to have two boys who truly enjoyed being with one another and kept each other entertained.

Even though he treasured playing with his brother and other friends, Derrick had the ability to enjoy playing alone too. He could entertain himself for hours with matchbox cars, action figures, or with his Tonka construction trucks in the sandbox outside. One of Derrick's favorite past-times was playing with his garbage trucks. He absolutely loved wadding up paper to stuff in his toy garbage truck as he played pretend 'garbage man.' In fact, as he got older he told me that he wanted to be a garbage man. I remember encouraging him to set his sights a little higher by becoming the owner of a large garbage company. He let me know in no uncertain terms that he did not want to merely be the owner—no, he wanted to be *'the'* garbage man. He religiously set his alarm clock very early once a week to make absolute certain that he would not miss the garbage truck's visit to our house to pick up our garbage. He was only around 8 years old at the time, and being the immature and naïve mom that I was, I would actually allow him to walk all alone down to the bottom of our very long driveway to watch and wait for the garbage truck. Of course, I would get a little nervous if he was gone too long, but knowing how much he loved doing this, I would let him go. Once in awhile, Travis participated in these early morning ventures as he tried to share his brother's immense enthusiasm for these very large and stinky vehicles!

On one occasion, my over-permissiveness turned into a very frightening experience. Travis had been with Derrick watching the garbage truck do its thing, and he returned to the house to let me know that Derrick drove off with the garbage man. "What do you mean he left with the garbage man?" I asked him. Travis informed me that the garbage man told Derrick that he would take him for a ride in his truck, so without hesitation Derrick jumped onto the back of his truck and they took off. I immediately told Travis to get into my car, and we frantically began searching the neighborhood for Derrick shouting and calling out his name. My son was nowhere to be found. I had absolutely no idea where to go. I began crying, and I was so scared that I would not find him. I eventually found him several streets over hanging onto the back of the truck like the big guys do. He was experiencing the ride of his life! He looked so happy and just beamed when he saw me. I know for certain that I totally burst his happy, little bubble as I scowled and yelled at him to immediately get into my car. I can't remember for sure what I did after that. I am quite sure, however, that he received the lecture of his life. I was so relieved that I found him, but so angry at the same time that he would take off with a complete stranger. Then again, he was so young and naïve. He meant no harm. The lure of these magnificent vehicles was just too much for a little boy to resist. He experienced the thrill of his life hanging on the back of that garbage truck, even if only for a short while.

I experienced this exploratory nature in Derrick on more than one occasion. I recall another incident when I experienced out-of-control hysteria after searching for some time for my son because he did not come home from school one day. Again, he was around 8 years old. On most days of the week Derrick and his brother were transported by bus to a local church after-school program. This routine happened four days a week on the days I worked, but on my day off, the boys were to come directly home from school. Derrick knew the routine well. One particular day Travis came home without his brother. He did not seem to know where he was either. I waited a little while, but before long, panic set in. Where could he be? I called the school. No Derrick. I drove to the church. No Derrick. Over an hour elapsed, and still no Derrick. With each passing moment, I became more hysterical. My husband came home from work, my in-laws made a surprise visit, and by now they all knew what had transpired. Lo and behold, a short while later Derrick came walking home totally oblivious to having done anything wrong. Mixed with relief and anger, I grabbed him to reprimand him. Once again, he did not intend to frighten me. In his usual independent nature, he decided to stop at the playground on his way home from school and play for awhile before returning home. One thing is for sure—he sure knew how to scare the living daylights out of his mom!

I have many vivid memories of Derrick, and one of them was how much he loved to eat. His favorite meal of all time was fish sticks, tater tots, and corn. He also loved fruit. When we would go to a restaurant for dinner, he would quickly make his way to the salad bar. He savored watermelon, pineapples and cantaloupes. He hated brussel sprouts with a passion, and unbeknownst to me, Travis would secretly eat them for him when I made them for dinner.

He loathed tight clothing, including blue jeans, but he sure loved his sweat pants. The funny thing is he always had to wear shorts under them or any other pants for that matter. He was sensitive, smart, witty, and strong-willed, but in a good way. Other than his few unapproved explorations, he was a very compliant child. He hated spankings, so he was a good listener and very obedient. He was very social and exhibited leadership qualities even at his young age. Because his birthday was in late September, we waited a year before sending him to school. Derrick was bright and confident and this showed among his peers. He had many friends, and was also quite the 'class clown.' Even though he excelled in school as academics came easy for him, I was often told that he would rush through his school work so that he could spend his free time drawing.

Derrick's passion was his artwork. He'd draw extensively—anywhere and anytime. He always had a notebook binder handy so that he would be prepared to capture an elaborate and intricate illustration of a moving vehicle, factory, or anything else that captivated him. He was good at it too. His little mind would take in all the small details that most eyes would miss. He would draw in vivid detail, pictures of trucks with their many cylinders and pistons. His illustrations completely amazed me, and I knew it was his special talent from God. I am so sure that with his love of drawing and attention to detail, he would have made a tremendous engineer or architect. Quite possibly, he would have been designing the latest garbage trucks or a state-of-the art garbage facility!

Derrick also loved traveling. I took the boys on a trip to Germany one year when they were 5 and 7 years old. They had an absolute blast. Of course the plane trip was quite the highlight. He enjoyed seeing another country, meeting his German relatives, and he dreamed of returning someday. He also kept record of all the states and special places he had visited. One place he dreamed of going to was Chicago to see the Sears Tower—at that time one of the world's largest buildings. In November of 1989, his dream came true. The boys and I visited my grandparents who lived in Illinois, and we took a side trip to Chicago. We drove by the Sears Tower; however, I was afraid to stop downtown on my own with two young kids. He did get to see it, but unfortunately not quite like he envisioned. He also dreamed of visiting other great landmarks such as the Statue of Liberty.

By far, the fondest memory I have of Derrick was his special connection to God. I do not even know where to begin or how to describe his love for the Lord. In fact, I was quite oblivious to it until much later. I do remember, however, his fascination with Jesus. He drew pictures all the time of Jesus hanging on the cross. Sometimes the two thieves would also be depicted on either side of Jesus. My birthday and Mother's Day cards would say, "I Love You Mom," and the illustration on the card would be of Jesus hanging on the cross. I remember thinking how sweet that he would always be thinking of Jesus, but I never really understood that he already had a unique relationship with God even at his young age. While I did read Bible stories to the boys before bedtime, I do not remember consistently talking to them about God. He attended a Catholic school, John XXIII, and I knew the children received religious instruction there. He had his First Holy Communion in the second grade and took this sacrament very serious. On one particular Sunday, as we were about to sit down on the pews, I noticed that Derrick knelt down, performed the sign of the cross, and said a prayer before sitting down. I never taught him that. Wow, I was impressed! In some special way that only he and God knew, Derrick encountered the

Lord in ways that I would not personally experience until I was much older. What a blessing that God hand picks little ones to come to know him personally. Who says that wisdom comes with age? In fact, I believe that God chooses these little ones, and reveals hidden things to them because of their innocence, humility, and childlike faith. Scripture confirms that God has a special connection with children. *"From the lips of children and infants you have ordained praise" Psalm 8:2.* Yes, indeed, Derrick and the Lord had a special relationship—one that I, too, would experience. However, not until I had been refined in the fire through immense pain and sorrow.

Dear Derrick,

Yes, my son, you were a very special child. I only wish I would have slowed down a little to savor you more. I was so new at everything and still so young myself. You were my first, and I know I expected so much of you. Forgive me for being so hard on you at times. Please know that you brought immense joy to my life, even if I did not know completely how to be a great mom. I know it did not matter to you that your baby items came from garage sales, and that your room was not decorated with the latest baby fashions. You were loved by us, and I knew that would suffice. Your father and I were so young and immature when you were born. Having you made us grow up quickly and brought such happiness to our lives as we experimented with this thing called 'parent-hood.' Thanks for being such a good sport and such a good kid.

You were also the best big brother Travis could have had. You know, Travis did not talk for a long time, but then again he didn't have to. He communicated to you in that baby language and you understood just what he wanted and needed. I know the two of you had a special bond, and I was happy you had each other. You truly made it easy to be a mom and to love you. Thanks, my dear son, for your easy-going, sweet-spirited nature. You were such a blessing to me.

Love, Your Mom

Brotherly love, Derrick & Travis, 4 and 2 yrs. old.

Derrick on his 2nd birthday.

Derrick fell asleep with his favorite book.

Playing outside with one of his toy trucks.

Derrick loved drawing constructions trucks.

The Break-Up   4

Turn to me and be gracious to me, for I am lonely and afflicted. The troubles of my heart have multiplied; free me from my anguish. Look upon my affliction and my distress and take away all my sins.   *Psalm 25:16-18*

Years seemed to fly by and my boys grew older. Though I loved them immensely, I was so incredibly starved for adult companionship that I re-entered the workforce. At first I started part-time, but by the time Derrick was 4 years old, I was a full-time working mom. I could not quite shake the guilt, however, of being away from the boys so much. Granted the extra money sure did help, but I knew deep in my heart that I should be at home with them. Selfishness and loneliness clouded my judgment, and I proceeded to find myself in the rat race of life. Maybe that is why time flew by so quickly. There was little time for savoring the small things in life. I did not stop to 'smell the roses.' My life was consumed with working, raising kids, and maintaining the home. Therefore, I went out of my way to make the weekends special. We did a lot of roller skating, movie watching, shopping, and having lunch at McDonalds. I also made sure the boys had opportunities to participate in sports. Even though Derrick joined a few to satisfy me, I could tell early on that it was not his thing. When I signed the boys up for art classes on Saturday mornings I could tell that I found his niche. This is where Derrick flourished. He was an excellent, detail-oriented artist if I do say so myself. I still have many of his drawings, and some are even framed and gracing the walls of my home. He was also quite a swimmer and loved being in the water. Travis seemed to enjoy all of the things his big brother did, if nothing else, to be close to him.

On Sundays the boys and I attended church together. There was only a cry room for babies, and preschoolers were expected to sit with their parents at the church we attended. That was okay, because for the most part, the boys were obedient and could sit still during church. Besides, it was important to me that they learn about God. I was thankful for my upbringing in the church, and I wanted to make sure that my boys had that foundation too.

Though my life was very busy with my full-time job and the raising of my boys, in the deep places in my heart, I was extremely lonely. My marriage was falling apart and it did not appear that my husband and I had much in common anymore. He had his hobbies and interests, and I had mine. Seldom did we delve into each other's activities or engage in meaningful conversations. It was almost as if we were leading separate lives even though we were still living under the same roof. Over the course of many years, we grew apart. Although we tried marital counseling, the distance between us only grew. They say that opposites attract, yet we were just two different people going in two very different directions. I was emotionally divorced years before the divorce actually occurred. The glue that kept us together for eleven years was our children. Finally, the glue could no longer hold us together, and I decided that it was better to live alone and be happy than to stay in an unfulfilled marriage. I knew this would be hard on the boys, but I also believed in my heart that everything would turn out alright. I would explain to them that it was not their fault and that their father and I loved them dearly and would continue to do so. Life would go on and we would find our own happiness, yet separately.

The boys handled the news quite well. I believe youth and innocence was on their side and helped protect their tender hearts. Their father moved out of the house, and their lives continued as normal as possible. They went to school as usual, and were able to see their father on a regular basis. In many ways, I believe their relationship with him actually improved as they mutually looked forward to being together and spending quality time with one another. He loved his children, and made the best of an otherwise bad situation.

Even though things appeared to be going well, I decided to let the boys' teachers know about the divorce. They were quite surprised as there was no evidence in their behavior that there was anything peculiar or abnormal going on. On the surface the boys seemed to be adjusting well, but deep in their hearts they felt the loss of our family unit, and maybe even suppressed the pain or longing for us to be together again. I worked at a law office for many years and was determined not to get into some of those nasty struggles with the ex-husband that so many of our clients got into. The only ones who ultimately suffered were the children. I vowed not to do that to them and I kept my promise.

After many months of living separately, on Monday, February 5, 1990, our divorce was finalized. It is amazing how a marriage can be obliterated so simply and quickly. Within a matter of minutes, the hearing was over and a marriage of eleven years was dissolved. It was all so surreal. We drove off in our separate vehicles, and I waved at him as my car drove past his on the highway. I returned to work and finished out the day. That afternoon, Derrick and Travis gave me a bouquet of flowers—small, pink carnations. A neighbor who periodically watched them after school must have purchased them for the boys.

I was actually in good spirits, and I had high aspirations that my life would be filled with happiness and adventure. The boys and I were going to be just fine. I would see to that. I was resolute that our lives would go on unaffected by this rather drastic change. I knew financially that I would be able to take care of us, and it was agreed that the boys and I would remain in the house. We both wanted to keep their lives as stable as possible. I was free to begin a new life for myself, and surprisingly, I had no angst about my future. I was about to embark on the biggest adventure of my life. There was no stopping me now. Little did I know, that within a few short days the exciting new life and adventure I anticipated would take me on a completely different course—certainly not the kind I had envisioned. And never the kind I would have hoped for.

Dear Derrick,

I want you to know how truly sorry I am that you had to experience the breakup of your family. I hope you know that it was not your fault. You did nothing whatsoever to cause this. Both your dad and I loved you and Travis very much, yet this choice that I made for us, no doubt, hurt you very much. Even though outwardly you seemed to adjust so well, I also know that your sweet spirit must have ached immensely to see your mommy and daddy split up. How on earth does a 9 year old process such a thing? I do not even remember explaining much to you about it—only that it was not your fault. What a sad example of a mom I have been. How could I have been so self-absorbed that I could look past the pain in a small child's heart? Everything changed for you when your daddy moved out. I am sure that your security felt threatened.

Please know that I never ever intended to hurt you and was very hopeful that you would adjust if you just felt love from both of us. I am sorry I did this to our family. I was not happy and I had great aspirations and dreams of making it up to you and your brother. We would be okay together—the three of us. Love would cover us all, I promise.

Love, Your Mom

Derrick, 4 years old, loved playing with non-conventional toys like Dad's pumps and car jacks.

"For my thoughts are not your thoughts, neither are your ways my ways," declares the Lord. "As the heavens are higher than the earth, so are my ways higher than your ways and my thoughts than your thoughts." Isaiah 55:8-9

Derrick came home from school glowing with excitement. He was invited by a school classmate to a 'Batman' birthday party. You have to understand how special this was to Derrick. You see, he absolutely adored Batman, and anything pertaining to or having to do with Batman and Robin was sure to be a hit. He not only loved the TV show 'Batman and Robin,' but all other Batman paraphernalia as well. The party would be held on Friday, the 9th of February, and involved a sleepover. Derrick was elated as he did not get to do this sort of thing often. I did not know the family well, but that did not matter. The boys went to a small Catholic school and denying him such fun would never have entered my mind. I was a young mom and simply did not deliberate over these sorts of matters. A birthday party? What fun! Of course I'd allow Derrick to go. Saying "No" never even entered my mind. He was absolutely thrilled and eagerly counted down the days until this special birthday party.

The day finally arrived, and Derrick excitedly came home from school that afternoon anticipating the great time he would have at the party. Late in the afternoon it began to lightly drizzle. When it was time to go Derrick asked me if I could give him a ride to his friend's house. Since his friend lived practically in our backyard only a short distance away I told him to just run there quickly. He agreed, we said our 'goodbyes,' and off he went running through the backyard. I told him to be home the next day by 10:00 a.m.

That next morning at around 10:00 a.m. the phone rang, and Derrick's voice was on the other end of the line. "Mom, it's Derrick. Can I please stay a little longer? I'm having so much fun." Once again, I found it difficult to say no to my child. "Sure Derrick, you can stay, but please be home by 2:00 p.m., okay?" I did not give a second thought to allowing him to stay a little while longer. He had not been to many sleepovers, and I was glad he was having such a great time. In the meantime, I would go to the local flea market with my friend, Carl, and Travis. After we returned home, Carl and I played Monopoly on the computer while Travis played in the yard with a friend.

A little while later around 1:15 p.m., I received another phone call. This time it was not Derrick's voice I heard. In fact, I didn't recognize this voice nor did I remember everything that was said. The only audible message that registered in my brain was that there had been an accident, and I was to go directly to Middletown Regional Hospital. That was it. I quickly hung up the phone, asked Carl to watch Travis, and headed toward the hospital. Maybe he fell out of a tree and broke a leg, or maybe he received a superficial cut from a tree branch. Yet inside my heart I could not shake the horrible feeling that something terrible was wrong. I'm not talking broken bones, cuts, scrapes or bruises, but something much worse. "Oh, please God, please. Please, let Derrick be okay." I implored God over and over during that five minute ride to the hospital to please let my little boy be okay.

I made it to the emergency room, and to my surprise he was not even there. I ran to the information counter, gave the nurse my name, and told her I heard there was an accident involving my son. She asked me to please have a seat in the waiting room and that he would be arriving soon. A few short minutes passed when an emergency vehicle pulled up. A stretcher with a body on it was hurriedly wheeled through the hospital emergency room doors. The emergency personnel quickly vanished out of sight with the stretcher, but instinctively I knew the body under this bloody sheet was my son. "Oh, my God, oh, my God, what has happened? Please God, please God, let him be alright."

The next several minutes were a big blur to me. To this day, I do not know the exact sequence of events that seemed to rapidly unfold in front of me. They came for me and I was escorted into a very small room. Various hospital personnel took turns entering the room and began talking to me. My body seemed to have a mind of its own. I began shaking uncontrollably. Even though I was sitting down, my legs were furiously trembling and moving up and down a hundred miles a minute. Time seemed to stand still, and it felt like I was in this room for a very long time. I kept asking if Derrick was okay. Everyone evaded my question, and no one seemed to know what had happened. Instead, they asked me how they could reach Derrick's father. I told them that he was staying at his parent's house.

They called my house and spoke to Carl. They called hospital clergy. They called the priest at St. Mary's Church. They called the hospital psychologist. In fact, many people were called. I did not know this at the time, but they were preparing to break some incredibly sad news to me and they wanted to be prepared. Everyone needed to be in the proper place.

Finally, the door opened and a rather large emergency room physician walked into the room with his head downcast, and rather bluntly said, "I'm sorry. You're son is dead." "What? How can this be?" I asked. He just shook his head, quickly offered his condolences, and then left the room. I began crying inconsolably as I have never cried before. No, I was wailing—tears of extreme anguish. "My baby, oh, my baby is gone." I remember thinking this cannot be true. They made a mistake. This is some horrible nightmare and I will wake up. This simply cannot be happening. Yet it was happening, and not in my dreams.

Someone was always with me, and one by one hospital staff tried ministering to me. Most of them just cried with me. There were no words that could bring a grieving mother comfort at such a time. They asked me if I wanted a shot to calm my nerves. I reluctantly agreed, and then I waited for Derrick's father to come. This was our son and even though we were no longer married, there was not a person alive who loved this child anymore than the two of us. When I saw him approach the emergency room doors I ran to him, hugged him, and cried out, "Derrick is gone." He was in utter shock although I do not remember him crying. We both asked to see our son's body. We needed to witness ourselves that our son was no longer living and breathing. Maybe they made a mistake.

We were both led into the room where Derrick's lifeless body lay. A white towel was draped over his head. Without hesitation I reached for the towel to look at my son's face when a nurse quickly grabbed my hand and asked me to please not look. I did not question her as my hand drew back and I obeyed her request. I continued to inspect the body. He was dressed in his favorite attire—a sweat suit. He had no socks on. I looked at his feet—yes, those were Derrick's feet and toes. I looked at his hands and the long slender fingers—

yes, those were his delicate, little hands. I held them in mine. They were still soft and pliable, but already yellowing. Rigor mortis had not yet set in. I remember thinking that this simply cannot be happening. This is the kind of fictitious story you read about in a book or watch on TV. Or it is something you hear about on the news and it always, always happens to someone else. Someone you do not know personally. This lifeless little body cannot be my own son. He was at a birthday party for heaven's sake, not in some shoddy part of town and the innocent victim of a violent crime. Yet without even looking at his beautiful fair-skinned face and big blue eyes, I knew this was my son. That was his lifeless body lying there. He was dead.

My body went into shock on that terrible day in February and that must explain why I do not remember so many details. I do have memories of certain people and events, but much of what happened in the days following my son's death still remains a mystery to me. The human body does incredibly amazing things, and my brain must have literally shut down to protect itself from all the gory details. Some memories I do have, other things I cannot recall at all. I was told that Derrick and another boy were playing in the elevator. The family had an elevator installed in a make-shift closet for their two handicapped sons. This elevator would allow them to freely get from one floor to the other in their wheelchairs. Unbeknownst to anyone, Derrick and the other children were playing in the elevator—innocently pushing the buttons and watching the elevator go up and down. How long they played in this elevator, I do not know. Only one child was still in the elevator with Derrick when the accident occurred. From what I understand, the protective gate that was previously installed was dismantled which allowed access to looking down the elevator shaft. Derrick was doing just that when the other child pushed the button and the elevator began to ascend. Derrick was lying facedown on the elevator floor looking underneath the elevator shaft as it began to slowly rise. He was, no doubt, totally enthralled and mesmerized as he watched all the pulleys do their wonderful work. He didn't have the foresight to know that he would have to move his head quickly before it reached the top portion of the closet door. The last few seconds of his precious life he was doing what he loved doing most—watching the intricate details of a mechanical pulley. He was, no doubt, storing up a mental image of his next detailed drawing of an elevator in action. Little did he know that there would be no place for his head to go once the elevator reached the top.

"Oh, dear God, my sweet little boy's face crushed beyond recognition." I had an exceptionally difficult time grasping how this accident occurred. I couldn't even fathom his perfect little face being distorted, and thankfully I refused to allow myself to linger there, for if I did, I knew that I would surely go insane. I thank God that he gave the emergency room nurse the foresight to place a towel on his head. The towel hid his disfiguration. I am grateful to the nurse who moved my hand out of the way and insisted I not lift the towel to view what remained of his face. I just know the image of seeing him in this way would have haunted me to my grave. To preserve my sanity, I simply could not permit myself to constantly think of what he must have gone through. If I did, these thoughts would surely torment me all the days of my life. I gave myself no other choice but to remember him the way he was, not marred by disfiguration, but as the beautiful fair-skinned, blond haired, blue-eyed little boy that he always was.

After awhile it was time for us to leave. A part of me wanted to stay there with him, and yet another part of me wanted to run as fast as I could far away from this morbid scene. I knew that his body had to be transported to the county morgue where the coroner would determine the cause of death. It was not necessary for him to perform an autopsy, nor would I have allowed it. The coroner determined the cause of Derrick's death to be 'cranio-cerebral trauma' due to an elevator accident wherein his head was pinned between the elevator floor and header.

Because the hospital staff insisted that I not drive myself home, my ex-husband drove me to my house, and my car remained at the hospital. We didn't say much. We were both in utter shock. He stopped halfway up the driveway, and Travis quickly ran up to greet us. He asked us if Derrick was okay. We then both knelt down to his eye level and told him that something very sad had happened. "Travis, Derrick died today. He will not be coming back because he is now in heaven with Jesus." We both tried to be so strong for him. He looked at us peculiarly as if his mind was trying to comprehend what we were telling him, and then barely shedding a tear said, "Oh, okay," as he turned around and ran back toward his friend to continue playing. That was it. Thereafter, my ex-husband left, and I began to walk up the long driveway toward the house.

Carl was standing outside waiting for me, and then our eyes met. I dropped my purse, ran into his arms, and sobbed uncontrollably. He held me so tight. He did not say a thing as all words failed him, so he did the only thing he could do—hold me and let me scream and cry. My friend and her husband were also there. Carl had asked them to come over after he received the call from the hospital. He was confused and scared and did not know how I would react. They stayed a little while and then went home.

A short while later, I went into auto-pilot and began to function quite normal. I knew there were phone calls to be made. Slowly and methodi-cally, I began to call family members who lived across the country. I also called a few of my local friends. They needed to know what happened. Carl kept on eye on Travis who appeared to be so unaffected by this devastating news. I tried to reach my parents in Texas, but they weren't home, so I called their best friends and gave them the devastating news. I called my sister, Rosi, who lived in Colorado at the time. She then called my younger sister, Monica, who lived in California. I called a good friend from work. I was very calm as I explained the horrible tragedy that had just unfolded—another indication that I was in complete and utter shock.

I am thankful for the periodic numbness that accompanied the shock. It enabled me to function and perform the necessary preparations for my son's burial. It would allow me to make it through the very difficult days that lie ahead. Looking back now, there are only a few things I vividly remember about the days following my son's death—masses of caring visitors stopping by to bring food and offer condolences, a woman from the church helping me pick out songs and scriptures for the funeral service, and the hardest part of all—going to a funeral home to pick out a coffin for my son.

Dear Derrick,

Oh, my sweet little boy. I can't even put into words what I am feeling now. I'm reduced to a puddle of tears just thinking about what has transpired in these last few hours. Did you have to

55

leave me, Derrick? Was it really your time? The only thing that brings me solace is that you were surrounded by friends, and that the last several hours of your life were happy as you were laughing, eating pizza, and having fun with your friends.

I can just envision you lying there on that elevator floor looking down the elevator shaft totally mesmerized. I'm sure your little eyes were trying to take it all in for this would be your next picture. You were an incredible young artist and every picture you drew had such precision and detail. You didn't miss a thing—every cylinder, every pulley, every nut and bolt. What your young mind could not comprehend was that when the elevator reached the top there would be no room for your head. If you'd known this, I know you would not have lain there so long. The law of gravity took over...there was something in its way...the engine kept working...and then you were gone.

What a horrific way to die! Please, please tell me you did not feel a thing. If you did, I will go crazy. No, you couldn't have. I am sure that Jesus would not have allowed you to feel such pain. In fact, he probably sent an angel to be with you in that elevator. Surely the angel took your hand and led you straight into the arms of Jesus. There must be a hoard of angels surrounding me right now because I cannot even begin to fathom how I will survive your death. I am in my own elevator descending into the depths of hell.

Love, Your Mom

Going Home 6

The righteous perish, and no one ponders it in his heart; devout men are taken away, and no one understands that the righteous are taken away to be spared from evil. Those who walk uprightly enter into peace; they find rest as they lie in death.

Isaiah 57:1-2

Breitenbach-McCoy Leffler Funeral Home—I found them in the Yellow Pages. I know that sounds so incredibly odd, but I did not have any prior experience on how to properly organize a funeral. After all, I had never buried anyone before—ever. I called and made an appointment with the funeral director. I was glad that Carl accompanied me to the funeral home. I was not prepared for the myriad of questions. Again, I was offered condolences. I could not see beyond my own pain to realize how many people were affected by this terrible tragedy. Even a funeral director who performed thousands of funerals could show immense sadness at the mere thought of the senseless death of a child. After he obtained all the necessary information, he led us down a hall and opened the doors to a huge room.

A surge of shock filled me anew and I realized I was in a showroom of coffins. Apparently I was expected to walk through this showroom to shop for a coffin for my son's lifeless body. I clung to Carl as I ever so slowly forced myself to walk through this vast room, carefully perusing all the different types of coffins that were available. I never knew there would be so many to choose from. Couldn't someone just pick one out for me? Was it really necessary for me to walk alongside each of these coffins, fully opened to display their various interior colors and satin fabrics? Being in that room made me sick to my stomach. I knew the funeral director was only doing his job, and surely he must have felt awkward watching this mother pick out a coffin for her young child. I was told that because my son was a tall boy I would need to pick out a full size coffin to accommodate his body. This was all so surreal. I could not linger in this room for another moment so I hastily picked one out. I remember very little about how it looked on the outside, only that the interior coverings were made of a light blue silk fabric. Since he was a boy, blue would work just fine. It had not totally registered with me yet that the next time I would see my son, his lifeless body would be lying in this very coffin.

A woman from St. Mary's Church arrived that Sunday afternoon. She was the volunteer that helped prepare the funeral service. She asked me to choose hymns that would be played at Derrick's funeral. I picked out a few of my favorite Christian songs—*As the Deer Pants for Water* and *On Eagle's Wings*—definitely that one. I loved the lyrics to that song. *"And I will lift you up on ea-gle's wings, bear you on the breath of dawn, make you to shine like the sun, and hold you in the palm of my hands."* Once again, the rest was a blur. I am sure she must have talked about other things too; however, my mind would not cooperate. I simply could not take it all in.

Shock was my companion on that day, the next, and for weeks afterward. In fact, it was my invisible friend, and it enabled me to make it through my son's funeral. I was relieved that I did not have to choose the graveyard where he would be buried—Derrick's father would do that. A close friend of his owned an excavating business, and together the two of them prepared the grave. I cannot even fathom picking up a shovel to help excavate the frozen ground on a cold February morning, but I was told that my ex-husband would help ready the gravesite. In fact, he insisted on do-ing so. Fortunately, we did not have to pick out the tombstone until many months later. Once again, I was grateful for that.

The funeral was to be held on February 14, 1990, four days after Derrick's death. It would take this long to prepare for the funeral, post the obituary in the paper, and perform all the other necessary arrangements. Those responsible for making the funeral arrangements had no way of knowing that this day also happened to be my 30th birthday. I insisted that my son not be buried on my birthday. From that day forward, my birthdays would only serve as a constant reminder of a very heartbreaking occasion. I pleaded with them to move it up one day, and fortunately, they obliged. On Tuesday, February 13, 1990, my son's body was laid to rest at the Miltonville Cemetery in Trenton, Ohio.

The weather was remarkably mild that day. It was not the usual cold, dark, dismal day that one would expect in February. In fact, the temperatures rose to the mid 60's and the sun shone brightly that afternoon. I believe it was God's way of smiling down on us. I am thankful that it was not rainy or gloomy for bright sunny days have a way of cheering me up. At least my son would be buried on a beautiful day.

I refused to wear the traditional funeral garb—all black. Out of reverence and respect, I wore a tea-length black skirt. Out of love for my son and to symbolize the sunshine that his life represented to me, I wore a bright yellow blouse. This was intentional. It did not matter what anyone else thought. With no makeup and bloodshot eyes from the incessant crying, I mustered the strength to drive once again to the funeral home where the day's events were about to unfold. Untraditional as it may be, I requested that the viewing, funeral service, and burial all be conducted in one day. I didn't want to prolong this event any longer than was necessary.

Extended family members arrived early, and this was the only time the coffin would be opened. For the remainder of the ceremony the coffin would stay closed. His father and I were the first to approach the coffin. I was terrified to look in it. Then again, I had to make sure that his body was indeed in there, that the clothes I picked out for him were on him, and that the blue and white gemstone cross that my parents gave me for my First Holy Communion was around his neck. We knelt down in front of the coffin, and I reluctantly looked in. A white towel was draped over Derrick's head. Thankfully, the funeral director saw to it that his face was covered. No one needed to see my precious son's deformed face. He was beautiful and that was the way he should always be remembered.

There was no mistaking that the body lying there was Derrick's. Everything was as I had requested. He had on his favorite Batman sweat suit. I was not about to bury him in a suit or some more 'appropriate' attire. Derrick was all about comfort, and he loved wearing his sweats. So, that is what he wore. The cross was around his neck. I reached out to touch his hands and they felt so peculiar. His hands were rigid and inflexible—not like they were at the hospital. The embalming fluid altered his hands to a mummified state. It was at that precise moment that I realized that the body lying there was no longer my son. This little body was nothing more than a 'shell' that once housed my son's precious spirit. As odd as that sounds, it brought me great comfort. I knew that the body being buried and going seven feet under the ground later that day was not Derrick. Derrick was already at home—his home in heaven with Jesus.

We asked Travis to view Derrick's body because it was important to us that he understood what had transpired. Even though he was still so young, it was a necessary process for Travis to go through in order to bring eventual closure to Derrick's death. He put a few of Derrick's favorite things in the coffin—a Batman action figure, a small garbage truck, and a few stuffed animals. What this innocent young child must have been feeling is inconceivable to me. Then again, so engulfed in my own grief, I was incapable of fully being there for him. That did not surprise God though. He poured forth an insurmountable amount of grace on Travis—not only on the day his big brother died and on the day of the funeral, but on every single day since then. In addition, He gave him the gift of a resilient spirit—and that is a gift that can only come from God.

A great number of people showed their support to me that day. The funeral hall was filled to capacity as people began waiting in line to offer their condolences. Either they came to the funeral home, attended the burial mass, or drove to the cemetery. Some were there for the entire day. Many of these people I had not seen in years, and some of them I did not even recognize. Stories were told of how our boys played soccer together years earlier or how they knew Derrick from some other place and time. It is indescribable how compassionate humanity can be in times of crisis and tragedy. I truly felt God's love being poured out through others that day. I had absolutely no idea how much the death of my son had impacted them.

The funeral hall was overflowing with fragrant flowers and beautiful planters. In my naivety, I mentioned to the funeral director how beautifully he had decorated the room where Derrick lay. I presumed that they were the ones providing the flowers. He proceeded to tell me that all of the flowers there were given by others in memory of Derrick to our family. A table was set up to display pictures of Derrick, as well as some of his beautiful drawings, writings, and favorite toys. Since there was no body to view, people needed something tangible of Derrick's to look at.

Rivers of tears were shed that day and heaven's floodgates were opened wide. I know the Lord was crying with all of us that tearful day. He felt our immense sorrow and pain too. Yet He knew something that we could not fully comprehend in such intense moments of grief and sadness. While we on earth were lamenting, all of heaven was rejoicing as Derrick was welcomed home.

Dear Derrick,

What incredible sadness has shrouded me these past four days. From the day you died to the day I buried your precious little body, I have been in a state of shock, experiencing so much, yet un-

able to fully comprehend it all. I must have aged tremendously these last few days as grief has painted my face. I know that it would hurt you to think of me in so much pain, yet I ask myself, "How can I not hurt?" You are my son and the light of my life, and I can't even grasp that you are no longer here with me. How can I possibly go on without you? I ask why this had to happen. Why? There are so many questions, yet so few answers. Maybe with time I'll understand a little better. Right now it takes all the strength I can muster to even think of life without you.

Did you smell all the beautiful flowers on the day of your funeral? And did you see how many people came to support our family? I know they were crying with us. The death of a child touches one in such deep places. You had lots of friends Derrick, and so many people cared for you. You will be missed so incredibly much. I know you would have wanted to wear your favorite Batman sweat suit. Travis wanted you to have a few of your special toys too, so he made sure to place them in your coffin.

My heart aches for you, but I have to be strong for Travis. So much has changed in our lives, and he needs me now more than ever. I know that Jesus will somehow, someway enable me to endure life without you. When you left this earth so suddenly, you left a void in my heart. Yet, I believe that all of heaven was rejoicing as they welcomed you to your eternal home. I will try hard not to cry—I wouldn't want you to be sad. After all, you are in heaven with Jesus, and I am sure there is no crying allowed. Please just ask Him to give me grace and strength to endure life without you. And don't worry, little one. Your momma will be okay. I promise.

Love, Your Mom

The First Days   7

"O Lord, do not rebuke me in your anger or discipline me in your wrath. Be merciful to me, Lord, for I am faint; O Lord, heal me, for my bones are in agony. My soul is in anguish. How long, O Lord, how long? Turn, O Lord, and deliver me; save me because of your unfailing love. No one remembers you when he is dead. Who praises you from the grave? I am worn out from groaning; all night long I flood my bed with weeping and drench my couch with tears. My eyes grow weak with sorrow; they fail because of all my foes." Psalm 6:1-7

The day after the funeral was my 30th birthday. My parents and my sister, Monica, stayed at my place for a few days. They had traveled across the country to be with me, and I welcomed their extended visit. As we gathered in the dining room to eat breakfast, my parents wished me a happy birthday and then in unison broke out in song, "Happy Birthday to you, Happy Birthday to you..." I asked them to please stop, but they ignored my request and continued to sing. It must have been extremely awkward for them to be joyous at this moment, yet in their pain they acted almost stoic as if nothing at all had happened. In fact, they appeared to be handling the death of their first grandchild quite well. Little did I know that they were trying to hold it together and be strong for me. I, on the other hand, just wanted to skip this birthday altogether, as it certainly was not a 'happy' birthday. The thought of celebrating it made me nauseous. Just yesterday I buried my 9 year old son. The mere notion of ever laughing or singing again seemed remotely impossible. Let's face it—my life had been forever altered. I had absolutely nothing to laugh or be happy about.

The doorbell seemed to ring nonstop for the next several days. Friends and acquaintances stopped by to bring food and offer their condolences. Surprisingly, I was able to eat. Besides eating, sleeping, and crying, there was little else I could do. I had absolutely no energy for anything else. It was as if all my previous vigor and energy had been stolen from me. I literally clung to Carl like a child who had just been reunited with his mother after a long absence.

I only received three days of bereavement leave from work. How on earth could they possibly expect me to return to work after only three days? Fortunately, I had not used my vacation leave for the year so I did not have to face going to work for a couple of weeks. During this time, Carl and I flew to Key West, Florida, for a few days. I had an insatiable need to get away from all the painful experiences I had just lived through. In my naivety, I must have thought that physical distance would in some way alter my state of mind or take away my sorrow. I soon found out that distance did not offer me any respite whatsoever. On the contrary, the pain seemed to follow me wherever I went.

Somewhere in southern Florida we changed planes and boarded a small ten passenger plane headed toward Key West. I remember looking out the window and seeing white, billowy clouds everywhere. Tears streamed down my face as I imagined Derrick jumping from one cloud to another all the while laughing and having a grand time. Is this what heaven is like? I tried hard to hide my constant flow of tears, yet I felt so weak, vulnerable and scared. This was all so surreal. Emotionally I was a wreck and in utter turmoil, but little did I know that my body was about to begin manifesting signs of acute stress.

We finally arrived in Key West and checked into our room. I quickly changed into my swimsuit and made my way to a lounge chair by the swimming pool. I remember how good the warm sun felt on my aching body. I dozed off for a little while as my body welcomed the rest. While I lay there daydreaming, I was oblivious to the damage the sun was inflicting on my body. Even though I was only in the sun for a short time, it was long enough to do damage. Later that day I could barely walk. My feet turned crimson red as they began to swell. I endured the pain thinking they would start to heal, but they only worsened with time. Common sense should have told me to go to a medical facility, but then again, I was unable to reason with any sort of normality. I endured the pain, and a few days later we returned home to Ohio.

Just two days later, we flew to Texas to visit my parents for a couple of days. By the time we arrived in Texas, I could no longer take a step without excruciating pain. The skin on my feet was extremely red, dry, and tight. With each step I took, it felt like a thousand needles were stabbing me. Had it not been for my wise mother who insisted on taking me to a local medical facility, I would have surely endured even more physical pain. I was hurting so bad emotionally, why not suffer physically too? The doctor and staff meticulously scrubbed off the dead layer of skin that had begun bubbling up and peeling. Although it was excruciatingly painful, I was relieved that I was finally receiving medical attention. My freshly scrubbed, raw flesh was coated with a heavy salve, bandaged up, and I was sent on my way. My diagnosis—second and third degree burns.

We only stayed for a few days with my parents. It gave them a chance to become better acquainted with Carl. Their first encounter with him had been at the funeral. Surprisingly, everyone around me acted fairly normal. After all, the funeral was over, and now it was time to get on with living, right? Although outwardly I appeared to be handling things fairly well, inwardly I wept and grieved uncontrollably for my little boy. My heart was broken. I wanted him back so badly.

What I would have done to go back in time to alter the events and insist he be home by 10:00 a.m. as I originally asked him to. Then none of this would have happened. "Oh, God, why did he have to die? Why? Was it because of my mistakes and failures? The divorce? I know I have been so selfish and sinful. Are you punishing me, Lord, for my sins? Did you have to take Derrick? Oh, God, please tell me why?" These questions churned around in my mind as I hopelessly clung to life one day at a time. It took every ounce of strength I had to even make it through one day.

  The time came for me to return to work. It was extremely difficult to go back to work and face my co-workers. What would I say to them? How would I act? No doubt, they had also rehearsed in their minds how they would approach me and what they would say. After all, what do you say to a young mother who had just buried her child? I learned so much about people through this sad experience. Most of them are undeniably kind and compassionate. Many will even put their own comfort level aside to approach you, difficult and uncomfortable as it may be, to offer a word of solace. And yet there are others who will bend over backwards to avoid you and the unpleasant feeling it brings them. Never mind that my world has been shaken so violently. A few people could not face me at all, and if by chance we suddenly found ourselves face to face, they would act as if their pretentious attitude or silence could alter the events.

"Let's just smile and not talk about uncomfortable matters," was the inaudible message I heard. Unfortunately, I lost respect for some of these people. They appeared to lack any sort of compassion, and I felt invalidated and disrespected. It was not until many years later that I learned sometimes human nature in its deliberate attempt to preserve face renders oneself unable to display any kind of emotion. It is simply too risky and uncomfortable for some people to do so. What a shame. I pity those who walk around stone-faced in an attempt to hide their true feelings. On the other hand, maybe they simply did not have the capacity to feel someone else's pain because they had never experienced anything traumatic or painful in their own lives.

In those early days after Derrick's death, I somehow managed to eat, sleep, and function. Though my heart was breaking inside, the reality of what happened had not caught up with my mind yet. They say the first stage you go through is shock. You are so numb and everything is so unbelievable, and it takes awhile for the facts to really sink in. I like to think of that as God's grace to the grieving. As the days turned into weeks, I would find myself waking up in the morning only to realize that I did not have a nightmare; that this was real; that Derrick was dead; and, that he was not coming back. My mind began playing dirty tricks on me as I was experiencing my own 'nightmare' every single morning when I awoke. Reality was about to become my new friend. As it slowly visited me morning after morning, its sole purpose was to torment me by reminding me that this terribly sad and distressing event really did transpire. It was not just some horrific dream. Derrick did die, and he was gone. Forever. Then the tears would flow all over again. How could I possibly go on?

Dear Derrick –

These last few weeks have been so hard without you. What I would do to have just one more day with you. It bothers me tremendously that I did not tell you I loved you when you ran out the door on your way to the party. You do know how much I love you, don't you?

I am filled with regret over many things. I am so sorry about the divorce. I know it hurt you terribly that your dad and I split up. Even though I have told you before, it was not your fault. Please do not think for a moment that you did anything wrong. I am incredibly sorry for all the things that I did that were not right. Many of my parenting choices were not the best. I was so young when you were born, yet I have no excuses. I know God has forgiven me, and I hope you do too. I have so much growing up to do.

This all seems so unreal to me. Did you really die? Have you left this world? I do not know how I can go on living without you. The memory of you is still so fresh. As I hold your red sweater close to my face, I can still smell you. I can still see your beautiful fair-skinned complexion, your big smile, and those beautiful, blue eyes. Tell me it is not real. You are just on an extended visit some-where. You'll come back to me, won't you? Please hurry, because I don't know how I can live without you.

Love, Your Mom

Derrick and Travis playing 'sandbox' in the kitchen with the pancake mix.

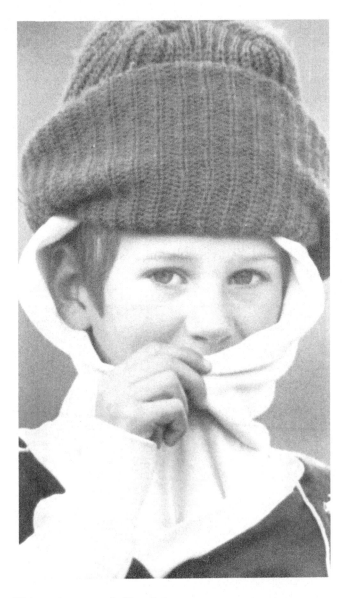

This picture of Derrick at a soccer game was printed in the local newspaper.

The Empty Desk   8

To comfort all who mourn, and provide for those who grieve in Zion—to bestow on them a crown of beauty instead of ashes, the oil of gladness instead of mourning, and a garment of praise instead of a spirit of despair. They will be called oaks of righteousness, a planting of the Lord for the display of his splendor.   *Isaiah 61:3*

During those first few weeks and months people from all over showered me with love and support. I am so thankful for the many condolence cards and letters of encouragement that I received. I knew that Derrick's death touched them all in a very profound way. Sufficient to say, it is sad indeed when a loved one dies, but when death takes the life of a child—well, the entire community grieves. It just seems so senseless, and everyone would agree that no parent should ever have to bury his own child. Ironically, others do not even have to know the child personally, yet they hurt anyway. They hurt for the family that remains; they hurt for the child who did not get a chance to live; and, they hurt for themselves and the possibility that it could happen to them too. Anyone who has had the privilege of being a parent is especially prone to immense sadness. Just the mere thought of it being his or her own child can reduce a grown man or woman to tears for someone they did not even know. I cannot recall how many people have told me over the years that they can't even begin to imagine the horrific pain associated with losing a child. People hurt for me—of that I am sure. Yet they could only go so far with that hurt because it left them feeling vulnerable and defenseless. They did what they could and the only thing they knew to do—send me a card, bring me a meal, and support me through prayer.

Though I appreciated every last one of them, one card I received impacted me in a very extraordinary way, and the words penned remain with me to this day. Over the years I was frequently reminded of this powerful message, and in some strange way helped me remain a mom to my 7 year old son, Travis. The ironic thing is these words came from someone that I didn't even know. She lived in Queensbury, New York, and had heard about the tragedy through a friend. She felt compelled to write me, and little did she know that her very words enabled me to set my priorities straight. I must not forget about Derrick's younger brother Travis, who in his own young way was also grieving the loss of his brother. She understood that grief would render me powerless at times because grieving is hard work. It takes energy, strength, and brute-force determination to not give up or totally fall apart. While you are grieving you are self-absorbed in your own misery. You are in the very pit of hell, totally encompassed with darkness and anguish of soul. It is a place that no parent should ever be, and would certainly never, ever ask for. While in this pit of darkness, it is quite easy and possibly even normal to forget everything and everyone else around you. Yes, including your spouse or any other children you may have.

After she expressed her deepest sympathy over my loss, she went on to briefly tell me a little bit about herself. She shared her story about her older brother who died in an accident while she was a teenager. Her loss was magnified because unfortunately, not only did her brother die, but her mother and father died too. Not a physical death, but an emotional one. They literally shut down as they were overcome by grief. No longer there for her, they ceased being the parents that she so desperately needed and had previously known. They stopped living when their son died, and for her they were as good as dead. Oh, my goodness— how incredibly sad to read her words. While it is natural to grieve immensely when a child dies, their son's death rendered them incapable of being a parent to their hurting daughter who still needed their love and nurturing. Not only did she need to grieve with her parents, but she hungered for their affection and for hope. Needless to say, she did not get that from the two people she loved the most.

The mere thought of being rendered incapable of being an effective and loving parent to the children who remain was just so perplexing to me. I vowed that although I would grieve for the child I could no longer hold, I would not be absent from the child who still needed me so much. This woman will never know on this side of heaven the impact her letter had on me. I thank her for reminding me that I am still living and I must live, if nothing else, for my remaining child.

Other handwritten notes and drawings came from the third grade class of John XXIII Elementary School, the school Derrick had attended. These scribbled letters and drawings were so precious to me. They were the friends Derrick held most dear. They were the ones who played with him, laughed with him, and loved him. A few of them were the last ones to see him alive. He had spent his final moments of life with them at the birthday party. Though I am sure they missed him immensely, I praise God for children's resilience. They don't process death in the same way adults do, and in many ways I believe they are blessed because of it. They seem to take things in stride and can accept with faith that their friend died, went to heaven, and is in a better place.

Even Travis was sad initially when we told him his brother died and shed a few tears, but I could see that he was incapable of fully comprehending what had just transpired. I remember on the day of the funeral how unusually well he functioned, and he just wanted to play with the other children who were present. When we returned home, he lay in front of the TV with some cousins playing his new video game as though nothing unusual had happened.

I very much wanted to visit Derrick's friends at school to let them know how much I appreciated their love and friendship to him. I made arrangements to visit Mrs. Glynn's third grade class and my mom and sister decided to join me. I can't remember exactly what I said to these children, but it was important to me that they knew how much I appreciated their friendship to Derrick. I also thanked them for their many cards and pictures. As I looked intently into their innocent little faces, I will never forget what I saw when my eyes caught sight of the empty desk—the desk Derrick sat in every day. On the desktop were flowers and two blooming planters. Mrs. Glynn told me that for the remainder of the school year the desk would be kept vacant in memory of Derrick. No one would be allowed to sit there for it was Derrick's desk. It was all I could do to keep it together for in my soul, I was wailing. What an incredibly heartbreaking sight! That was Derrick's desk, the place where he sat day after day. Those faces staring at me were his dearest friends—the ones he laughed and played with and spoke of so often. How can it be that his desk is now empty? Full of life and vigor, it was only a few days ago that he was sitting in that vacant desk.

Experiences such as this were reminders to me that something in my life had altered drastically. Sympathy cards, letters, flowers, an empty desk, and a vacant room—one by one these tangible reminders awakened my soul to the realization that my little boy no longer lived here.

Dear Derrick,

People have been so good to me these last few days. They are literally coming out of the woodwork. People I do not even know are sending cards and letters to encourage and comfort me. These acts of kindness are so appreciated. My refrigerator is overflowing with food. I have not cooked a meal in so long and I don't know if I even remember how to. Inherently, they must know this for they are dropping by and bringing all kinds of casseroles and desserts.

One thing I felt compelled to do was visit your classmates, and so I did a few days after your funeral. I needed to see your friends because I know they are hurting too. How confusing it must be for a third grader to play with his friend one day, and the next day be told that he cannot play anymore because he is now in heaven. Children, on the other hand, seem to take these sorts of things in stride. Maybe their tender spirits are somehow spared from feeling immense sorrow. Or maybe we adults have got it all wrong and need to have their 'childlike faith.'

When I entered your classroom it was still decorated for Valentine's Day. Construction paper hearts were everywhere, and I was given your bag of Valentines from your classmates to take home with me. Did you see how many pictures, cards and notes your friends made for me? I have saved every one of them in a special box. I cannot bear to part with them just like I can't bear to part with your special toys, the ones you so loved playing with. It is as if I can still see you playing intently with them making all those brrrm, brrrm sounds that little boys make when they play with their trucks and cars.

It is unbearable for me to walk by your room everyday. Sometimes I stop to peek in and I see your bunk bed and dresser and all the little things you held so dear in the exact place they were when you last touched them. It is especially difficult to look into your closet where your clothes are hanging. Your school uniform and your favorite sweaters are all still hanging there. I touch and smell them hoping in some way to feel close to you.

I dread the day when I must go through all your things, one by one, for I know it will be excruciating to handle them and finally store them away. I know often people decide to keep their child's room just as it was when he died, but I know that I will not be able to do that. It is just too painful to look into your room and not expect you to come walking in at any moment. No, I cannot do that for if I do, I will deny myself the realization that you

are gone and are not coming back. I will, how-
ever, display some of your personal items through-
out the house as a constant reminder that although
you may not be here physically, you are still here—
living in my heart.

Love, Your Mom

Derrick's 3rd grade class and the empty desk with flowers on it.

Who am I?
I love to swim. I like GI Joe.
I have captain power and
Lazer tag I like Tuesday
mornings. I have blue eyes
and I love buzzes. I like Batman and I love to draw
and my birthday is Sept 21.
Now Who in the wold am I?

One of Derrick's assignments in 3rd grade.
Who Am I?
I love to swim. I like G.I. Joe. I have captain power and Lazer tag. I like Tuesday mornings. I have blue eyes and I love buzzes. I like Batman and I love to draw and my birthday is Sept. 21. Now Who in the world am I?

Strengthen the feeble hands, steady the knees that give way; say to those with fearful hearts—be strong, do not fear; your God will come, he will come with vengeance; with divine retribution he will come to save you. Isaiah 35:3-4

C arl reached his hands out to me and said, "Diana, here take my strength." Even though I heard everything he said I was incapable of taking any strength from his hands. I tried—I really did. My hands felt like limp rags. As strange as it sounds, I tried to hold his hands to squeeze them tight, but was unable to. It was as if all energy and strength had been zapped from me. I was such a pitiful sight to behold. What must I have looked like from his point of view? In retrospect, he must have felt so useless, so incredibly sad for me, wanting so much to help, yet incapable of doing so. At times I wondered what made him want to stay with me. After all, I was a frail and pathetic mess. He often told me that there was something special in me, and that he could somehow see beyond the pain I was in to the woman I would become. I think God gave him a glimpse of the future—He must have, because the turmoil I put him through surely must have made him question why he ever committed to staying with me.

Carl was an angel in disguise sent by God. I believe with everything in me that he was sent for 'such a time as this' to be the heart that loved me, the hands that held me, and the arms that picked me up when I collapsed. Carl was truly being Jesus to me. He showed such genuine love and compassion, and this type of unconditional, agape love can only come from God.

On one occasion when I thought my heart would burst out of its chamber, I took a bubble-bath hopeful that soaking in its warmth would ease the pain of my aching heart. Carl came home from work and heard me sobbing. The piercing sound of my cries led him to the bathroom where he found me weeping inconsolably. I will never forget what he did next. Fully clothed, he stepped into the bathtub, sat behind me, held me tight, and proceeded to sob with me. What a sight the two of us must have been! We cried for what seemed like an eternity. He allowed himself to feel my pain in a way that no one else around me did. For this I was thankful. I knew that he was vicariously journeying with me on this painful path. It hurt him too. He was the closest one to me, and he felt it too. At work I had to put on a façade, but at home my mask came off and I was allowed to be authentic. When I thought of Derrick, or heard a song that reminded me of him, or saw a piece of watermelon or cantaloupe or other food that he loved to eat, it was as if a knife twisted in my heart, and fresh blood, sweat, and tears could simply not be contained. The floodgate had just broken again and tears spilled forth by the gallon. Carl allowed me to grieve the way I needed to and often his tears accompanied mine.

I cannot recall how many times he picked me up off the floor. Grief zapped every ounce of strength I had. Sometimes my legs would just give out, and I would collapse on the floor right in front of him. He would pick me up, lift me to my feet, and hold me until I felt strong enough to stand. Sometimes I collapsed outside, sometimes in the house. It didn't matter where I was, and I never knew when it would happen. We were always alone though. I felt safe in his presence.

Time and time again Carl would hold out his hands and plead with me to take his strength. Invariably at these times I was also uncontrollably crying. He must have felt so utterly helpless. It was not until many years later that I stumbled upon the significance of this single and 'holy' act. In countless places throughout the Bible it talks about taking Jesus' strength through His mighty hands. Little did Carl or even I know back then that Jesus was right there with us manifesting himself to me through Carl's loving hands.

Dear Derrick,

Do you see all my tears, my little one? I sure hope not because if you do, undoubtedly you will be sad too. My tears have become my daily food. They are flowing like streams of water in a dry and parched land. I can't seem to control them either. They come and they go, whenever, wherever. Every little memory of you triggers another downpour. I especially find it hard to go to a salad bar. Remember how much you loved eating fruit? Especially watermelon, cantaloupe, pineapple, and honeydew. A part of me wants to savor them like you did, the other part of me just wants to pick them up and throw them across the room. Or when I pick up the toys that you so loved playing with— Batman and Robin figures, GI Joe's, and garbage and construction trucks. As I hold them close, I remember your little hands holding them too. You spent countless hours playing with these little toys. They brought you so much pleasure.

You know what seems so strange? After I have cried my eyes out I feel so drained, yet refreshed and better. What a paradox! I know in some strange way it is necessary for me to grieve like this. After all, I loved you so much. How can I not cry for you now that you are no longer here with me? My body is writhing in agony. Every bone in my body is rebelling. Rebelling against what has happened. I so desperately want you back. I think that is why my body is fighting so hard. It just isn't fair. "What good can come out of this pain?" I ask myself.

Where are you now? Are you in heaven with Jesus? Do you see me? Just in case you do, I will try to pull myself together. It's bad enough that one of us is hurting so. I can't bear the thought of you hurting too.

I do want you to know how special Carl has become to me. He must be an angel in disguise—seriously! I know you only saw him a handful of times. He has stayed by my side. He cries with me, and he picks me up off the floor when I collapse, and he does this really peculiar thing by holding out his hands and asking me to take his strength. He loves me in a real deep and profound way. Why he puts up with my constant emotional turmoil is unbeknownst to me, but I need him now Derrick. I do not know how to go on living without you, and I am grateful that he is there for me. So I will try to take his hands, hoping that in some way they will give me the strength I need to carry on without you.

Love, Your Mom

Mind and Body

*Be merciful to me, O Lord, for I am in dis-
tress; my eyes grow weak with sorrow, my soul and
my body with grief. My life is consumed by anguish
and my years by groaning; my strength fails because of my affliction, and my bones grow weak.*
Psalm 31:9-10

He is not coming back. Why does it
take so long to grasp that fact? *Hope
deferred makes the heart sick (Prov. 13:12).* Not
only was my heart sick, as the days turned into
weeks and the weeks turned into months, the
physical manifestations of grief were now quickly
beginning to wreak havoc on my body. I guess I
never realized how much the mind and body are
connected. As my soul was hurting my body felt
the pain too. Unusual and strange things began
happening to me—things that just do not happen to
an otherwise normal and healthy person—second-
degree sunburns, chronic bladder infections, and
ulcers, to name just a few. Every flu bug and virus
decided to attach itself to me too, and that first year
without Derrick, I began to experience a deteriorat-
ing physical decline in my otherwise healthy body.

A few months after Derrick's death, I began experiencing stomach and esophageal upsets.
Everything I ate seemed to come up my esophagus,

and I began experiencing acid reflux. I had frequent stomach upsets, and my family doctor told me that it was imperative that I find another outlet for my grief because I was beginning to develop ulcers. I also caught every conceivable cold, flu and virus that was within a 100-mile radius! It was almost as if my body said, "Hey, I'm over here. Come and latch onto me."

Another source of trouble for me was chronic bladder infections. I had never before experienced a bladder infection so I had no idea how incredibly painful they were. They would come up so suddenly without warning and land me in a physician's office begging for medication. One particularly painful episode occurred as I was flying home after visiting my parents in Texas. When I left their home I felt some discomfort in my lower abdomen, but little did I know that within two hours I would be in such excruciating pain that it would be necessary for the pilot to radio control tower to request an ambulance upon my arrival. I sat in my seat shaking uncontrollably as my kidneys released their toxic poison. I did not think that I could survive this horribly intense pain. Immediately upon landing in Dallas, I was taken by ambulance to the local hospital for treatment. I missed my connecting flight to Cincinnati but that didn't matter. I just knew that I could not have endured this pain for another two hours. I compared it to childbirth labor pains—no even worse.

That first year without my son, not only was my heart broken, my body was broken too. Never in my life had I suffered so many illnesses and ailments in such a relatively short period of time. Even worse than being physically sick, I was tired of constantly feeling sick. Now I had not only a broken heart but a failing body too. When will this suffering end? Will it ever end? Internally I confessed that I could not continue to go on like this. I was not living—I was barely surviving. Something had to give or I would just wither away and die. This slow, debilitating, and exhausting illness seemed to ravage my body. What used to function with relative ease was now being severely sabotaged as I struggled to keep my physical body from harm. Wasn't it enough that my very soul was in such turmoil? Did my body have to experience such agony too? I found out that the two go hand in hand. What affects the body will eventually affect the soul, and what affects the soul will eventually affect the body. They truly are intertwined and you can't isolate them from each other.

Furthermore, the profuse crying and hopelessness I felt was beginning to take its toll on me. It was as if I could emotionally not take one more day. God must have known I had reached my limit because one morning was a little different. I cried out in agony. This consuming pain had to cease or it would kill me. I lay there in bed contemplating my life. Although I did not want to get out of bed, I knew I had a choice to make. I could physically, emotionally, and spiritually wither away and die, or I could choose to live and find new purpose and meaning for my life, despite the pain and suffering. God inaudibly spoke to my spirit that morning. After evaluating my choices, it didn't take long for me to make up my mind. I was tired of being sick; tired of uncontrollably crying; tired of collapsing on the floor; tired of nightmares; tired of physical weakness; tired of being helpless; and, above all, tired of feeling hopeless. I did not know how this would all play out, but on that day as my feet touched the floor, I chose to live. I chose Him. I could hear Him speak to my spirit, "Diana, one step at a time. One day at a time. Do not try to figure out tomorrow, or next week, or next month. Just take my hand and let us make it together through this one day. Tomorrow, we will do it again, and the next day again."

God let me know in a way that I could understand that He would be with me and would help me face my todays and tomorrows. Looking back, that was a huge turning point for me. Although sickness still came and afflicted my body for the next two years, it did not defeat me. I had no outward tangible sign that God was with me, yet intrinsically, I knew that He was the one carrying me and giving me the strength to live.

Dear Derrick,
    I am reminded every morning when I awake that you died and are not coming back to me. Al-

though I am trying to comprehend this bitter truth, my body is screaming for you. I have been sick a lot lately. You know how I hate being sick. I was never good patient. My life exemplified the epitome of health. Not anymore. I have had the craziest things happen to me and have landed in the hospital on more than one occasion—all because of the stress of losing you. I never knew how stress could affect the physical body. Now I do.

Something really cool happened to me one morning, Derrick. Jesus spoke to my spirit. I know it was Him. It had to be. I was so tired of hurting, crying, and feeling hopeless. I heard God's Spirit whisper to mine, and He told me to take one step at a time, one day at a time with Him. You see, I could have so easily given up on life. But you would be proud of me. I chose Him, Derrick. I know God is big and powerful and almighty and in some way He will help me make it through this life without you. How? I am not quite sure. But I do know that I must trust Him. My very life depends on it.

Love, Your Mom

This picture of the boys and I was taken while on vacation in Colorado.

Derrick and Travis while on a family camping trip.

Derrick's first day of school entering 1st grade.

How long, O Lord? Will you forget me forever? How long will you hide your face from me? How long must I wrestle with my thoughts and every day have sorrow in my heart? How long will my enemy triumph over me? Look on me and answer, O Lord my God. Give light to my eyes, or I will sleep in death; my enemy will say, I have overcome him, and my foes will rejoice when I fall. But I trust in your unfailing love; my heart rejoices in your salvation. I will sing to the Lord, for he has been good to me.   *Psalm 13:1-6*

Another psychological phenomenon that I experienced was the 'fight or flee' syndrome. Because I am not much of the fighting kind, (in fact, I am known to be a peacemaker), I seemed to exhibit the 'flee' part much more readily than the fighting part. I had such an intense desire to flee or run away from the intense anguish I was in.

Even though I had made up my mind to take one day at a time, and I knew that in some mysterious way God would help me; however, some days the pain of not having Derrick with me intensified. Those were the days when something else inside of me took over. It was something dark and even though it was evil at its very core, I was lured to it. It was a strong pull away from anything good or of God, and it seemed to take my soul on a quick downward spiral into the depths of despair. I believe it was the enemy of my soul—Satan's evil spirits, and they enjoyed tormenting me. For clarification, I will name this evil force Darkness.

When Darkness came, I felt invariably helpless as if I had no control whatsoever. Thoughts would invade my mind and soon my body followed by acting on these very destructive thoughts. One such event happened about five months after Derrick's death. Carl had taken me and my sister, Rosi, to Sanibel Island in Florida. Once again, he did what he does best—he tried to bring pleasure and beauty into my life. He exposed me to so many wonderful places, yet my pain seemed to follow me wherever I went. It did not matter that we were vacationing on a beautiful island.

While in Florida on one particular day, Darkness reared his ugly head as he began tormenting me again. Could I not have even one day of reprieve? Did he have to follow me around everywhere I went? Even on vacation? Carl rented a catamaran and took us sailing in the ocean. It was great fun, and the three of us were laughing and carrying on as we cut through the waves. We were about a mile offshore when we noticed that the storm that had been brewing in the distance was now noticeably closer. As we made our way back to shore, the storm overtook us with rain, thunder, and lightning. Fortunately, we made it back to the beach without being struck by lightning. At this point it was raining very hard. Carl quickly helped the attendant pull the catamaran to a safe location. Without any warning, Darkness enveloped me and his voice ordered me to run. "Run fast into the deep, blue ocean and swim far, far away. Escape from this pain for no one cares about you anyway. No one understands you. Run to your son." Emotionally I resisted, but physically I obeyed the command to run. It was as if my body had a mind of its very own. I jumped to my feet and began running toward the ocean. As my feet touched the water, a surge of adrenaline allowed me to frantically begin swimming as fast and far away as I could.

My sister quickly ran after me and followed me into the deep water. She finally caught up to me, and I noticed that we were both sobbing uncontrollably. Carl remained onshore watching in horror as the two of us swam further into the ocean. He knew that sharks lurked about, but my sister and I did not give that a second thought. In fact, she began begging God to take us to Himself, to please just let us die right then and there. Suddenly something in me snapped and I realized how far away we had swum from the shore. I implored her to swim back with me and we made it safely to shore. It was one of those crazy moments when I simply did not know what I was doing. A force stronger than me coerced me into doing the unthinkable—trying to take my own life.

There were other times like this. That first year and a half, Darkness convinced me that alcohol would help me cope with my sorrow so it became my drink of choice. Usually one drink led to another and then another. Under the influence, I would find myself doing the most incredulous things. At first I would be happy and exhilarated—a common side effect of drinking alcohol. The next moment I would try to jump out of a moving vehicle. It was as if I would once again lose control of all my senses. Granted, I know that alcohol is a depressant, but is it depressing enough to make me do such crazy things?

I recall another episode when Darkness began whispering suicidal thoughts to me. "Why are you putting up with this? You know it hurts. Just put an end to your misery." I had just parked my car inside my garage and closed the door. Instead of turning off the ignition, I remained sitting in my car contemplating my miserable life. Darkness was right. It would feel so good to be free from the continuous emotional distress. After a few moments, I gained control of my senses and immediately turned off the ignition. What was I thinking? How could I even consider taking my life? Why was I being tormented so?

Deep down in my soul I did not want to give up on life, yet there was no denying that a piece of my soul died with Derrick. Even though our bodies were separated from one another physically, our souls were still connected. I recognized that I simply could not let my enemy win. I could not and would not take the easy way out. It went against everything I stood for and everything I believed in. I would be doing Derrick the biggest disservice of my life by giving up and what a cowering act that would be. He would not be proud of me for that, and I would not be proud of myself either.

Other times Darkness made me angry and I would put up a fight. Unfortunately, Carl was usually the recipient of my unfair outbursts. I would rant and rave and scream and tell him that he just didn't understand me at all. After all, Derrick was not his child. How could he even pretend to understand the pit of hell I was in? Carl became my personal punching bag and although I did not touch him physically, emotionally I often hurt him very deeply. Like the time in Florida at the restaurant when I picked up silverware and threw it at him. Yes, Darkness had me take it out on the ones I loved the most. Maybe Carl would not be able to handle my outbursts and then he would leave me too. Oh, how Darkness would love that. Then I would truly be all alone, and no one would be there to pick me up off the floor or keep me from jumping out of moving vehicles.

Other intense emotions seemed to flare up at the most inopportune times and I felt completely powerless to do anything about them either. Fortunately, there is One who is not powerless. He was doing the fighting for me. The battle was truly

His and He was fighting for my very soul. He was not going to let Darkness win. I belonged to Him and He knew that there was a battle waging against my flesh and soul. He wanted nothing more than glorious victory for me, but He also wanted to equip me with armor—all the tools necessary to keep Darkness from tormenting me—to keep him away from me altogether.

My flesh was weak and worn out. My senses were dulled. I was not living—I was merely surviving one day at a time. God wanted so much more for me. He wanted me to live again, but He also knew that I needed divine intervention. I needed power from above, and that was help only He could offer. Being the Omniscient God that He is, He knew just what I needed. Because I was not listening for His voice and was consumed with my sorrow, He knew what it would take to reach me. But first I had to surrender my son back to God. I had to release the tight grip I had on Derrick. I did not want to let him go, but my survival depended on it. My health was rapidly spiraling downward, and my emotions were on a roller coaster ride of their very own. Derrick's birthday was rapidly approaching, and God was at work in my heart—even if I did not feel or see any evidence of it.

Dear Derrick,

I would really like to believe that you can't see a thing that is going on down here. If you did, you would surely be ashamed of your mom. Why is

she acting like that? Does she not know how incredibly happy I am here in heaven? It's as if I
cannot help myself. I hurt so much and I want to
run from the pain. Other times I have such rage
inside of me and it just has to come out. I have
never experienced such a roller coaster of emotions in all of my life. There are times when I am
truly doing okay, believe me. Then a memory of
you comes to me which triggers an intense emotion. Darkness makes an appearance and leaves
me with tormenting thoughts—thoughts of how to
escape the pain. I know this Darkness that visits
me is the enemy. There is a war going on, Derrick.
A war is waging against my very soul. God is
there. In fact, He is fighting the battle for me as I
am a weak and wounded soldier. He knows that
without His divine intervention, I will not win
against this dark and strong force. I know He is on
my side, and therefore, I know I will win, even if it
doesn't seem like it. I have not given up, Derrick. I
will be okay, I promise. Please don't give up on
me either.

Love, Your Mom

Up, Up and Away 12

*To you I call, O Lord my Rock; do not turn
a deaf ear to me. For if you remain silent, I will be
like those who have gone down to the pit. Hear my
cry for mercy as I call to you for help, as I lift up
my hands toward your Most Holy Place.*

Psalm 28:1-2

Seven months after Derrick's death
would have been his 10th birthday.
Wow, double-digits! Most children can't wait until their first double-digit birthday. It must in some
way mark a new beginning for them away from
childhood into the pre-teen years. Isn't it ironic
that children can't wait for their birthdays to mark
another year on the calendar while adults wish they
could skip them altogether! This was a special
birthday and it would not go by uncelebrated. Although not here in the physical realm, Derrick was
with me in every other way. How could I ever forget my son's birthday? He was the first one to
make me a mom and I would never fail to commemorate that special day when he was born—
ever.

On my way to the cemetery I stopped by a
store to pick up some helium-filled balloons. After
all, what is a birthday without balloons? I had previously picked up some silk flowers to lay by the

little cross that marked his grave. His father and I still had not picked out the tombstone. I wanted to be alone so I went by myself. I drove to the cemetery on that warm, sunny September afternoon with my silk flowers and bouquet of balloons. What I was going to do with them I did not know. I just knew that he needed balloons and I would provide them.

When I arrived at the cemetery no one else was there. Derrick was buried in an old cemetery nestled on the outskirts of town. It was a very quaint looking cemetery filled with huge oak trees, and I seldom saw anybody there. I liked that it was so private because then I could cry or scream or do whatever I needed to do without an audience. And that is exactly what I did that day. I talked to Derrick, I cried for him, and I screamed out in agony, because no parent should have to celebrate their child's birthday in this manner. I was so thankful that I was the only one at the cemetery because my agony was overwhelming and could not be contained. Acutely aware of my surroundings, I experienced every conceivable sensation known to man. How could I feel such intense love and joy, pain and sorrow, anguish and despair all at the same time?

Seven months after Derrick died, I tasted death once again. This time I was present not only in the flesh, but with all mental faculties as well. When Derrick's body was laid to rest at this very cemetery seven months prior, I was not fully cognizant of what was transpiring. Although present physically, shock prevented me from attending the funeral mentally. As shock and denial began to subside, reality allowed me to taste death once again before I could finally surrender. It was healing for me to be there on that day with Derrick, my flowers, and my balloons. Not only was I commemorating my son's birthday, I was giving him back to God.

Completely caught up in emotion, I began to rapidly run through the cemetery like a dog off a leash, balloons in my hands, wailing at the top of my lungs, "I give him back to you God. I give him back." And then it happened—I let them go, one at a time. I released the tight grip on my hands as I watched them fly away, higher and higher into the atmosphere. I whispered to Derrick to please catch the balloons, and I told him that I had not forgotten his birthday, nor would I ever forget. As they slowly disappeared from my sight, I envisioned them making it all the way to heaven into Derrick's little hands. He would have a big smile on his face—that was for sure. I lingered there a little while longer before I decided it was time to go home. Ironically, I felt much better, and certainly relieved that this day I had dreaded had finally arrived and was coming to an end.

I had survived Derrick's first birthday without him. Little did I know at that time that this symbolic gesture of sending balloons to him in heaven would become my yearly ritual. Every year on his birthday, I show up with balloons—usually three. One gets fastened to the vase by the tombstone, and the other two I let fly as I stand there fixated on them until they are no longer visible. I visualize Derrick receiving them as a token of my love and continued devotion to him. On a deeper level, it is a continual symbolic act of letting go and surrendering him back to God.

Sometimes I bring balloons on February 10th, the day Derrick died. Why would I do that? Doesn't that imply that I'm also celebrating his death? Not at all. For many years I dreaded this day most of all. It was almost as if I relived the day he died over and over again. Shortly after Christmas and until February 10th, I would sink into a deep sadness that is hard to describe. The closest thing I can compare it to is depression. Considered a mood disorder, usually depression has no known cause. But this deep sadness that I felt—well, let me just say that I knew what triggered it—memories.

Hoards of Memories. Memories of Derrick as a baby and a little boy. Memories of his sweet, sensitive nature. Memories of his incredibly intelligent nature and his fun-loving personality. Memories of his last birthday party. Memories of the phone call. Memories of arriving at the hospital only to be told that my little boy was dead. Memories of seeing his lifeless body lying on that gurney with a towel draped over his face. Memories of the funeral and those stiff hands. "Oh, God, how can I ever forget all that has happened?" The same memories of Derrick that were so precious to me and that I savored above all also had the power to haunt me at other times. How can memories be so wonderful, yet so incredibly agonizing at the same time? What a paradox!

To make matters worse, these winter days were usually gloomy, wet and cold, and often the sun would hide its smile from humanity for days at a time. Even though February was a month of many birthdays—Carl's was on the 6th and mine on the 14th, it was very difficult to find anything to celebrate or be happy about. I felt as if I was betraying Derrick by being festive at this time. This gloomy month is the month when he died and that is what February would be remembered for—not birthday celebrations. What do I have to celebrate anyway?

The six weeks leading up to the anniversary date of his death were unusually difficult for me. I would sob incessantly, but not in front of others—I became a 'closet' crier. I hid my tears from the outside world, because innately I knew that they would not understand. In fact, they would probably think I am not dealing with this very well at all, and that by now I should surely be 'over it.' However, as one year led to another, I began to realize that you just don't 'get over it.' Then again, others would not understand so my tears were reserved for Derrick and me alone. I have since found out that grieving is a very solitary and isolated experience. You have to go through it alone. Sure, there are others around who try to understand and offer support, but ultimately they cannot take the experience away from you. Like it or not, you simply have to go through it—to feel the pain and anguish, and to cry and scream if need be. There is simply no other way around it. When I would mask my feelings and bottle them all up inside, it only seemed to exacerbate my emotions. My emotions were like a dam ready to burst, and it was only a matter of time before they spilled over.

Many years later on the 10th anniversary of Derrick's death, God gave me a new perspective about this day that I felt so anxious about year after year. He helped me find something positive about this extremely sad day to keep myself from constantly living in a state of trepidation for the six weeks leading up to it. I knew that my focus had to change and I had to find something good about this dreaded day. He began to whisper to my heart. "Diana, on this day Derrick may have left earth and been taken from you, but on this day he entered into paradise and he has been with me ever since. So you see Diana, February 10th is really his spiritual birthday." Wow! I never thought about it in that way before. In reality, that is so true. February 10th is the first day that Derrick saw Jesus face to face and the day he was reborn into God's heavenly kingdom. It is his birthday—his heavenly one. God sent me a blessing on that day, and since then I no longer feel anxious or apprehensive about the days and weeks leading up to February 10th. God gave me His perspective, and it sure was better than mine. That is certainly worth celebrating with balloons!

Dear Derrick,

Happy Birthday my precious 10 year old boy! How did you like the balloons? You know Derrick, on your birthday I did something that I didn't think I could do—I gave you back to God. I had to or I would not be able to survive. Please do not misunderstand me. I will never, ever forget you or stop loving you. I will never forget your smile, your sensitive nature, and I will never forget to celebrate your birthday, even if you aren't here with me physically. What I mean is that I gave up any right that I had to keep you here with me. That would be selfish, wouldn't it? I said goodbye to dreams about the young man you would become, and I said goodbye to all the dreams I had for you. You now belong in heaven with God. Earth could not hold you back and neither can I.

I'm sure that you must have had the biggest birthday party ever in heaven. I can picture you on the seat of honor with loved ones all around celebrating your life. Are the angels flying about and singing in harmony? I'm sure it is a birthday party quite unlike one you have ever had here! You know I always tried to make your birthdays special. They were always a big deal when I grew up and I wanted you to feel special too. I hope I succeeded.

I miss you, Derrick, so terribly much. Sometimes I believe that my heart is breaking into a thousand little pieces. Even so, reality tells me that I have to take care of myself so I can be strong for Travis. He still needs me. He is just a little guy himself. I know he misses you, too. You were his playmate and his best friend. He has suffered such loss this last year, and I hate that this little boy has to suffer so. So for his sake as well as my own, I had to release my grip on you and give you back to God.

I am slowly beginning to realize that you were His all along, not mine to hold onto. Why He brought you to Himself so soon I still do not know. In fact, there is a lot I don't know or understand. I just know that my body is crying out for relief from the roller coaster of emotions and physical manifestations that are beginning to take its toll on me. I must believe and trust that God has a plan for my life and in His time, He will reveal it to me. Right now I will just rest in Him and in those whom He has so graciously given me to love. I will continue to celebrate your life for you are still with me.

Love, Your Mom

This picture of Derrick and me was taken in April
1989 on his First Holy Communion.

Anxiously waiting for the garbage truck to come.

Derrick on his 9th birthday with Travis and friends.

Then your light will break forth like the dawn, and your healing will quickly appear; then your righteousness will go before you, and the glory of the Lord will be your rear guard. Then you will call, and the Lord will answer; you will cry for help, and he will say: Here am I.

Isaiah 58:8-9

The enemy continued to come in like a flood and threaten to destroy me. I knew that my weakness needed God's might and strength, and my safety depended on letting Him fight the battle for me. After all, He is very much acquainted with grief. In His mercy, He allowed all earthly comforters to fail me, and that by turning to Him, I may find everlasting consolation. Only He would be with me always, seeing everything and feeling every emotion that I did. Only He had the power to transform me and change my outlook. I could not depend on others to do it for me, but most importantly, I could not even depend on myself. Had it been up to me I would have certainly wallowed in my pain and died a slow, deliberate death. A part of me believed that I did not deserve to live. How could I when my young innocent child was denied his right to live? I was much more sinful and selfish than he ever was. He was just an innocent little child so pure in thought and deed. He did not do anything wrong. On the contrary, he was so sweet-spirited, caring and gentle. "Why, God, would you want him back? Isn't he just the type of person you need down here in this sin-filled world? Caring and thoughtful people who love you? Why would he have to return to you so soon? And why would I have to stay here struggling to make any sense of this tremendous loss? Why not take me? I'll take his place if you just let him come back."

I could not make any sense of it at all. The only thing that came to mind was that maybe God was punishing me. Punishing me for the divorce, punishing me for not being the parent I should have been, punishing me for my sinfulness. It would take a miracle from God to transform my pain and give me a reason to even want to continue to live. All I wanted to do was be with Derrick— even if it meant that I, too, had to die. Far too many days the only thing that stopped my mind from spiraling downward and doing something crazy was the realization that another precious little human being depended on my surviving this tragedy. And that little person was only 7 years old.

Instinctively, I knew this child still needed his mommy very much. His entire life was altered drastically in the last five months. First his parents separated and divorced, and now one of his best buddies, his big brother, was gone. What on earth must have gone through his little mind? God's grace flooded his little soul because he seemed to take it all in stride. He became almost obsessed with playing video games. Maybe this was his form of escape.

As Carl committed to remaining by my side, Travis seemed to accept Carl's place in my life. Of course, his loyalties belonged with his dad, but he found acceptance in his heart for this new person who was obviously so very important to me. He was not jealous or resentful, but embraced him as a friend. I was so appreciative that he accepted Carl because I clung to him as my sole means of emotional support. Furthermore, I was amazed at the resiliency that Travis seemed to possess. Rightfully, he had every reason to become defiant or even disrespectful. He could have failed at school or had issues with friends, but he did not. He continued to be such a blessing to me and unbeknownst to him, he was the primary reason I chose to live again. He was my 'ray of hope.' I couldn't allow myself to give up as my feelings often dictated for he still needed his mommy very much. I couldn't disappoint him for he had been through enough trauma to last a lifetime.

In reality, I was a poor model of what an effective parent should be. So caught up in a grief that threatened at any moment to swallow me whole, I knew that I was not fully present in my role as his mother. Physically I was there, but emotionally I was unable to lay aside my pain and be the mom he deserved to have. Gone were the days when I would take the kids rollerblading or to the matinee. Gone were the days of silly laughter when I would tickle the boys on my bed till they couldn't laugh anymore. Gone were the days when Travis and his brother would play for countless hours with action figures. Gone were the days of asking questions of his big brother believing that somehow he had all the answers. His life changed immensely, and now he became the only child of grieving parents who were often caught up in their own pain-filled worlds. Many happy days were behind him, and what loomed ahead was definitely unknown and unchartered territory.

I regret that Travis' life was not the kind of life a child should have had. So much pain inflicted on such a young child is just not right. No doubt, I did try to be the best mom I could be, but I also know that I failed miserably. When he should have been disciplined I was unable to do so, as I tried somehow to make up for this terrible wrong that he had experienced. Travis, however, didn't lack a thing materialistically as he had two homes filled with toys and the latest electronic gadgets. But then again, 'things' can't take away the pain.

About six months after Derrick died, Travis' father even bought him a boxer puppy whom he named Boo. This little dog meant the world to him. He loved and played with him whenever he was at his dad's house. I can't recall how long he had him—maybe four months at most. His dad lived on a main street and one day the puppy ran from the front yard into the busy street. In front of his own eyes, Travis saw his puppy get hit and killed by a car. How devastating it must have been for him to witness this tragedy. A few days after this accident, I found him lying on his bed crying uncontrollably. He had a picture of Derrick in one hand and a picture of Boo in the other. He was looking at both of these pictures and crying his heart out. I was heartbroken as I saw him filled with such pain. I tried to console him, but was only reduced to tears myself. What can you say to a little heart that is grieving so? I had no words, no explanations. Life just is not fair sometimes.

Once again he didn't talk much about the pain of losing his puppy, just like he didn't talk much about losing Derrick. I know that a lack of words does not indicate a lack of feeling. He must have internalized a lot of the pain. I am certain that his immature mind didn't quite know how to deal with the magnitude of such loss, so he kept his feelings to himself. It was very important to me that Travis not forget his brother so I talked about Derrick all the time. His father insisted that he meet with a counselor, and he was under a psychologist's care for about a year. He drew a lot of pictures and whether or not this helped him, I do not know for I never heard much about what took place in the counselor's office. Some things his father handled as he felt led to, and other things I did. Although we acted independently, we certainly had the same goal in mind—the well-being of our son, Travis. One thing is for sure—he had two parents who loved him very much and would try to be the very best parents possible under the difficult circumstances we were dealt. No, it was not the ideal life for a 7 year old boy. Deep in my heart I still believed that as long as he felt loved, he would survive the trauma. I am very grateful that he continued to have a great relationship with his dad, and he also had Carl and me. We all loved him deeply, and hopefully that was good enough.

Dear Derrick,

How you must ache in your heart for your little brother. One day you were playing action figures with him, the next day you were gone. Do you remember how well you two played together? He loved you so much. Do you have any idea how much he looked up to you? The two of you had your own language. Instead of asking questions of me or his dad, he would always ask you. He just knew that you had all the answers.

Do you remember how you guys would get up early on Saturday mornings to play GI Joe's? I'd ask you to play quietly so I could sleep in, and when I awoke I'd find the living room furniture slightly rearranged with ropes strung everywhere, as you were deeply immersed in GI Joe land. Or you'd play Batman and Robin. Of course, you were always Batman and Travis was Robin. We'd rummage through clothes to try to make you both look authentic. And how can I ever forget the pancake incident? You were both so young, maybe 2 and 4 years old. You were quietly playing in the kitchen, and when I checked on you, I found an entire pancake box strewn on the floor as you were playing sandbox. Somehow I just think that was your idea! Squealing in sheer delight, the two of you had the time of your life! Thankfully, instead of getting angry due to the big mess, I ran for the camera and made it a 'Kodak' moment. What a picture that was! I'll never forget it as long as I live.

You know I never had to arrange many play dates for you because you had your very own playmate with you always. Travis was all too eager to be with you, even if it meant you could boss him around a little. He didn't care—just being with you was all that mattered. Contrary to what usually happened in families concerning sibling rivalry, when you two argued, you did so politely and quietly. There was no screaming or hitting or punching. On one occasion when you did have a little spat, I remember ordering you both to take it outside because I didn't want to hear it. You were in the cold for a few moments, and I think the shock that I'd do such a thing made you instantly stop your arguing. Was I cruel when I did that or was it really child psychology at its best? I am sorry for handling it that way. I didn't always do the right thing, I know.

Even though Travis is so young, I will make sure that he doesn't forget you, Derrick. How he is coping with all of this is beyond me. It absolutely must be God's overflowing grace poured on him. He is doing okay, really. Please watch over him, and ask God to send angels to watch over him too. The future is so uncertain and only God will ever be able to make any sense out of losing you.

Love, Your Mom

Derrick absolutely loved to draw—especially any thing to do with Batman, construction trucks, and Jesus.

Derrick's picture of
'Batman'

The Secret Chamber   14

"Come to me, all you who are weary and burdened, and I will give you rest. Take my yoke upon you and learn from me, for I am gentle and humble in heart, and you will find rest for your souls. For my yoke is easy, and my burden is light."   *Matthew 11:28-30*

I had surrendered Derrick to God. I had my ray of hope, Travis, who was the sunshine in my life, and I had a wonderful friendship with Carl—who despite my many mood swings and outbursts chose to stand by my side. Even so, it became increasingly apparent to me that no one or anything could ease the constant state of internal pain I was in. Although not visible on the outside, inwardly my soul was perishing. I became disillusioned with people. Friends who I thought would always be there for me abandoned our friendship. Those who remained did not constantly want to hear about the pain of losing my boy. They were busy carrying on with their own lives. Although I know they wished me only the best and showed periodic concern, they were unable to identify with my sorrow. No one understood what I was feeling. Not even those closest to me. How could I expect them to?

I felt so incredibly isolated in my pain. I never knew anyone who had lost a child to death. There was no one I could turn to who could give me advice or assure me that what I was feeling was completely normal and that it would get better. Except, of course, the local grief group—which I did attend on two separate occasions. Rather than make me feel better, I wanted to run out of that meeting as the participants shared their own traumatic stories and then discussed in detail all the stages of grief I still had to go through. No thanks. That was too much for me to handle. I felt like I was singled out for this horrific loss and could not understand why God would allow me to continue to suffer.

Even though I loved Carl immensely, he began to fall short too. Internally, I was often very angry at him—probably because he was the closest to me and it was safe to be mad at him. He should have seen my pain for it was written all over my face. He should have felt my shattered heart break to thousands of pieces. I am sure he felt powerless to help me and frequently just said nothing at all. Nothing was even worse than something. Why couldn't people recognize that? Just say something—anything for heaven's sake. Lack of words was my silent killer. Instead, people just carried on like nothing had ever happened. Or they avoided me altogether. Maybe they were afraid of bringing up such an unpleasant topic for fear that I would fall apart. It was obvious that I made them feel uncomfortable, and so the time came for me to put on my mask. This mask would hide my pain from the outside world and would enable me to function. Furthermore, it would allow people to approach me again, because I looked normal with this mask on. After all, it is very uncomfortable to approach a person who looks down trodden and pitiful.

The mask enabled me to function on my job and interact with others, but in the privacy of my home I could take it off. I tried not to cry too much in front of Travis and Carl because I knew it hurt them to see me constantly crying. Over time I decided it was best to withhold my tears from their sight too and I became a 'closet crier.' Now I would only feel safe to cry when completely alone. Then the floodgates would open and a dam of tears would release. I always felt so much better after a hard cry. In a strange sort of way it was cleansing. I ached for the child I could no longer hold. The tears were my way of letting him know how much I missed him.

What must God have been feeling as He looked down to see me drenched with sorrow? I may have been able to hide my tears from others, but I could not hide them from Him. He saw every tear I cried, and I believe He cried with me. He ached for me to turn to Him, because He knew that only He could bring ultimate healing to my broken heart. He also knew that I must come to Him and that He would not force Himself on me. So He waited patiently for me day after day. But in His silence, He was hard at work—working on my broken heart. Although He knew I would have to feel additional pain through the disappointment of others, He was interceding on my behalf as He was patiently waiting for me to come.

I knew I reached the end of my resources. Nothing else mattered. I could not continue to pretend that I was alright. I was not alright. It did not matter what others thought of me either. It did not matter to me if they would run the other way because I had reached my limit. I needed a miracle, and I needed it from God. I recognized the state of my desperation and I now knew that I needed Jesus more than I needed anyone else.

Just as the high priest in Old Testament times would enter the Most Holy Place, I recognized that I, too, must enter into the secret chamber alone. I needed to be alone with God away from distractions, other people's opinions and viewpoints. I needed to hear from God Himself, and the only way to do that would be to enter into the secret chamber alone. I had received tremendous comfort from others, but I needed healing. And healing was something that others could not give me. Believe me I tried. I went to others expecting the unexpected. What was I thinking? How could anyone possibly feel what I felt and bring healing to my broken heart? God let me know that my healing would come from Him alone. I believe that is why He allowed me to face disappointment and continued turmoil. He was not trying to add more pain to my already broken heart. It was as if he formed an invisible and mysterious wall around me where he cut me off from others. Their words no longer brought comfort, their outward actions toward me no longer satisfied. He shut me up to Himself, to something divine, which was something new and unexpected. He gave me such an awareness of my need for Him. The things of old no longer pacified me, and pleasant memories of days gone by no longer sufficed. My soul survival depended on something new and different, and yet I did not know what or how it would come to pass. God is the Master Potter and it was time for him to make something out of this lump of clay. He no longer allowed anything or anyone to satisfy or take His rightful place. It was time to come to Him, and I had to come alone.

It was in the secret chamber of isolation that God would deal with me. With an open Bible in my hands and a constant flow of tears streaming down my face, it was there that He would personally meet and speak truth to my aching spirit. Alone with Him, away from the clamor of the world, He would breathe new life into my parched and weary soul. Detached from anything outwardly and clinging inwardly to Him alone, He was able to begin doing what He does best—perform miracles. It was His intention to do so all along yet was unable to. How can this be? He is God. He could have just said the word and I would have been healed. In His wisdom, He allowed the things of this world to fail me as He waited for me to become desperate. Desperate for a new vision for my life, desperate for healing, but most of all—desperate for Him. He was there all along patiently waiting for me. He knew that the lessons I needed to learn and the healing He wanted to impart would not stick until I was ready.

Dear Derrick,

I've been feeling very much alone lately. Kind of like being in a room filled with people, yet still feeling so isolated. Even though there is noise and laughter, I am not a part of it. I may be present, but I am so far, far away. It still amazes me that I can be sitting in a room with others as they laugh and carry on, and yet no one can see my heartache. It is as if a big knife is protruding out of my heart, but they simply cannot see it. Maybe the only ones who can are those who have also buried their children. I haven't met any of them yet. That may be another reason I feel so alone—like I've been singled out to experience this devastating tragedy. I did attend a grief group, but did not feel good there either. In fact, I am not really sure where to go to feel good, so I just put on a mask and pretend that I am okay. Maybe that is what others want to see.

I have discovered the only place I can be truly authentic is at home. In my desperation, I am beginning to look for God. Surely He is here with me and sees me. I think I was beginning to suffo-

cate those I loved the most by placing heavy bur-
dens on them. It was time to find a different place
to go to be real. I think God is a big God and He
can handle my cries, questions, and burdens. He's
got to, because I sure can't.

Love, Your Mom

Derrick (second from left), Travis (far right), and
their friends. Sept. 1987

Save me, O God, for the waters have come up to my neck. I sink in the miry depths, where there is no foothold. I have come into the deep waters; the floods engulf me. I am worn out calling for help; my throat is parched, my eyes fail, looking for my God.   *Psalm 69:1-3*

Though I was desperate for healing, time was not my friend. It would not stand still for me as one month after another seemed to pass by. Before I knew it, I had survived many 'firsts' without Derrick. Not only his birthday, but Christmas, New Year's Day, the one year Anniversary of his death, Easter, and all the other special holidays we used to enjoy celebrating. It slowly began to sink in that no amount of time would heal my wounds. Still very much a 'closet crier,' with each passing day I began to realize that I was in a very real hell all on my own and even though I cried out to God, I did not know how to climb out of that deep, dark pit. Reality sunk in that I was journeying in this dark place all alone. Friends stopped asking how I was doing, encouraging cards ceased to arrive in the mail, and everyone presumed that I was doing just fine. After all, over fourteen months had passed since Derrick died. Besides, I had recently married Carl, moved to a new town, quit my job, and started my new life.

Even with all this positive change, the pain in my heart intensified as painful memories continued to follow me wherever I went. There was just no getting away from them. As much as I loved talking about Derrick, others decided it was better not to talk about him. Maybe they were afraid I would cry, but couldn't they see my invisible tears? A deep sadness covered my soul and though I cried out to God for help, it appeared that my cries fell on deaf ears. What else could I do to escape the turmoil? No matter where I went or what I did, this deep sadness followed me. What was wrong with me? I had so much to look forward to. I was newly married to a wonderful man who truly was like a rock to me. Not only did he love me, he loved Travis too. He vowed to take care of us both even though he was very well acquainted with my sorrow, as well as my uncontrollable emotions and outbursts. Surely he must have known what he was getting himself into. Regardless, he promised to remain with me through it all.

Other exciting things also began to unfold in my life. We purchased a new home in a suburb of Cincinnati, and because I was able to quit my full-time job, I could pursue my lifelong dream of attending college. I was embarking on an entirely new life, and surely this life of new beginnings was a positive step in the right direction. I was amazed at God's graciousness to me. At times I was very happy, but under the surface the lingering deep sadness remained. It was always lurking around waiting for an opportune time to once again launch me into a state of intense mourning. How dare I be happy? My son was dead. He never had a chance at life. All the things he ever wanted to do never came to be. He wanted to see the Statue of Liberty. He wanted to travel the world. He wanted to get married and have two children. He wrote a paper in his class just weeks before his death stating these very things. Well, not one of them will ever be! So how can I possibly find joy in my life when my little boy was denied his?

Fortunately, thoughts of taking my own life no longer seemed like a suitable option. Instead an almost apathetic attitude emerged. As the shock and denial of losing Derrick wore off and reality set in, I began to feel hopeless—like this new life would never be what it could be. No matter how hard Carl tried to lift my spirits, no matter where we went on vacation, or what fun and exciting things we would do, I could not be lifted out of this sinister and bottomless pit. I was sinking in the mire and my soul was drowning. Physically I was present and functional, yet inwardly in the deep crevices of my soul, I was in a hell of my very own. I was in a dark, cavernous valley and the enemy of my soul, Darkness, was quite content in keeping me there. In fact, he delighted in my anguish and wanted nothing more than to watch me succumb by my own destruction.

This second year without Derrick was by far the most excruciatingly painful year for me. As shock, denial, confusion, anger, and bargaining with God had all come and gone, I was left with the blunt reality that Derrick was gone; that this was not some horrific nightmare; that God would not raise him from the dead as he did Lazarus; and, that he was never, ever coming back to me. No, I will not, I cannot ever be the same happy, free-spirited woman again. My life was dramatically altered in a way that I detested immensely, and I slowly began to drown in my own sea of tears.

None of this surprised God. He saw the continued anguish and despair of my soul. The cry of my distress rang in His ears. He knew that it was time—time for His divine intervention. He had watched Satan torment me with destructive thoughts and actions before. He saw the state of my soul and He saw my heart. He witnessed every single tear and heard every cry for mercy. Enough was enough. I had been in the pit for almost a year and a half and it was time for Him to supernaturally intervene. He would not allow Satan to torment me any longer. God gave me a gift that would save my life. One night while I was asleep He visited me in my dreams. I experienced first-hand the manifest presence of God through this dream. It was so vivid and real that when I awoke, I distinctively knew that it was a message from God. It was a message that would alter the direction of my life. It was my very own 'reversal of destiny.'

In my dream I was standing on the banks of a deep sea and I was all alone. I was at the point of no return. In my reality I could not foresee a future without Derrick. I simply could not live another painful day without him. I longed to be with him, and I desperately needed to flee from my life of pain. I noticed the sea was unusually different in that it was not peaceful or serene, nor did it have a shoreline that gradually grew deeper. No, this was a turbulent sea with fierce, torrential waves. Ironically, I was not afraid, and the time had come to end my life. The roar of the seas beckoned me. Without any hesitation, I plunged into the rushing torrent. The waves and the breakers crashed over me, and immediately I began thrashing around as I was quickly overtaken by a whirlwind of tumultuous waves. I cried out in agony. The waves were so fierce that I quickly began to drown.

And then it happened. The heavens parted and a massive hand reached down from the clouds and gently scooped me up and placed me on dry land. I screamed out, "No!" because I did not want to be rescued. I once again jumped in determined to end this life of pain. Immediately the waves began to drag me under, but the massive hand appeared once again and gently scooped me up a second time and put me on the spacious, dry land. I looked around and noticed I was all alone in this vast open space. This time I did not jump in again.

I awoke from the dream and began crying. Instinctively, I knew this dream was from God. The hand that rescued me was God's mighty right hand. I understood with absolute certainty that this was a divine message directly from God Himself. Carl awoke to my crying and through tears I described to him in vivid detail my dream. It was as if a veil had been lifted from my eyes, because I understood exactly what God was communicating to me—I was drowning in a sea of pain and sorrow and could not see a way out. I wanted to put an end to my suffering. The enemy of my soul was too strong for me. He was represented as the violent sea, the storm, and the thrashing waves. He beckoned me to join him as he seduced me into thinking that I could escape the pain if I just jumped in and ended it all. He knew the utterly hopeless and helpless state I was in. So I heeded Darkness' tantalizing voice. I truly felt that I had no choice but to give in and succumb to death—if not a physical one, then a spiritual one.

But God would not allow it. He knew I was being tormented and He understood that I saw no way out. He also knew that it was the right time for His divine intervention. I had already surrendered my son to Him. Now it was time to surrender myself. He would not permit the enemy to destroy me or thwart His plan for my life, for I was His child, and my name was engraved on the palm of His mighty hand. God would personally step in to rescue me from the mud and the mire and the bottomless pit I was in. He literally parted the heavens and reached down from on high to take hold of me. He miraculously intervened because I was in such a desperate place. My heart was shrinking as it quivered under the intensity of its suffering. The flood waters were beating down upon my soul. My heart was overflowing with a pain too deep for words as it began to shrivel and die inside its deepest chambers. But that was not God's sovereign plan. *"I know the plans I have for you," declares the Lord, "plans to prosper you, and not to harm you, plans to give you hope and a future" (Jeremiah 29:11).* In His sovereignty, He knew what my shriveling heart needed that weary night, and that is exactly what He delivered—supernatural and divine intervention.

Without a shadow of a doubt, my spirit connected with His on that dark night and I knew that God was going to save me. He was going to set me free from my enemy whose constant torment threatened to overtake me. He was going to do so because He loved me and because He had plans for me. Drowning in a sea of sorrow was no longer an option. From that day forward, I truly believed in my heart that I would survive Derrick's death. I did not know how God was going to liberate me, but it did not matter. He revealed Himself to me in a dream and by faith I believed in Him. Now, it was time for me to trust Him. If He could do His part and leave the throne room of heaven to come and save little 'ole me, then I had better do my part too. I would not let Him down. This dream was a continual reminder of God's mercy and grace and even though I may not have understood the full significance of it and how it would play out in my life, what my mind was able to comprehend was so very real to me. Maybe no one else would understand or even believe that it was a dream from God, but that did not matter to me either. I was not crazy or losing it. I knew it was God. I believed He was going to save me and that was really all that mattered.

Many years later, God through his magnificent grace confirmed to me in His Word my exact dream. As I began to pour over Scriptures, I found my dream documented in Psalm 18. It was written by King David and is a psalm of gratitude for deliverance and victory. It explains that the only sure way to be delivered from surrounding evil is to call upon God for help and strength. I could not believe what I was reading. There it was in the Bible—my very dream! God's goodness and mercy overwhelmingly reduced me to tears. Yes, God speaks to us in very real and sometimes miraculous ways. He met me at my lowest point in my greatest time of need, and revealed Himself to me in a way that I could identify. Years later when I could fully comprehend the magnitude of it all, He gave me the mercy of confirmation through his written Word.

Psalm 18:1-19 says," *I love you, O Lord, my strength. The Lord is my rock, my fortress and my deliverer; my God is my rock, in whom I take refuge. He is my shield and the horn of my salvation, my stronghold. I call to the Lord, who is worthy of praise, and I am saved from my enemies. The cords of death entangled me; the torrents of destruction overwhelmed me. The cords of the grave coiled around me; the snares of death confronted me. In my distress I called to the Lord; I cried to my God for help. From his temple he heard my voice; my cry came before him, into his ears.*

The earth trembled and quaked, and the foundations of the mountains shook; they trembled because he was angry. Smoke rose from his nostrils; consuming fire came from his mouth, burning coals blazed out of it. He parted the heavens and came down; dark clouds were under his feet. He mounted the cherubim and flew; he soared on the wings of the wind. He made darkness his covering, his canopy around him—the dark rain clouds of the sky. Out of the brightness of his presence clouds advanced, with hailstones and bolts of lightning. The Lord thundered from heaven; the voice of the Most High resounded. He shot his arrows and scattered the enemies, great bolts of lightning and routed them. The valleys of the sea were exposed and the foundations of the earth laid bare at your rebuke, O Lord, at the blast of breath from your nostrils.

He reached down from on high and took hold of me; he drew me out of deep waters. He rescued me from my powerful enemy, from my foes, who were too strong for me. They confronted me in the day of my disaster, but the Lord was my support. He brought me out into a spacious place; he rescued me because he delighted in me."

Wow! I learned from the Word of God that 'drowning in deep waters' is powerful imagery that symbolizes great distress and sorrow. Only God has the power to rescue and subsequently redeem us from such tremendous troubles and distress. Going through these rivers of difficulty will either cause you to drown or force you to grow stronger in the Lord. If you go in your own strength, you are more likely to drown. If you invite the Lord to go with you, He will protect and rescue you. It became apparent to me that all of this time I elevated Carl to a place that he should not have been in my life. I expected him to take away my pain and sorrow. I expected him to be my rock and my savior. Now I understood that God allowed me to experience extreme disappointment in Carl and others so that I would turn to the only One who could truly help me. I was slowly suffocating Carl by requiring so much of him—requiring things that only God could give me. Although I was thankful that I had Carl's strong shoulders to cry on, I began to realize that I needed to lean on God, not on a mere mortal. For who is like God? There is no one like Him. He alone could save my soul and redeem my life from the pit.

I intuitively knew that it was time to go back to church. It must have been God's Spirit beckoning me. It had been almost two years since Derrick died, and shortly thereafter I stopped going to church. It was too painful to attend church, and I was reduced to a flood of tears the few times I did go. I remember actually running out of church one time—I just could not take it. I did not know which church to go to for we had since moved to a new town. Nothing surprised God for He knew exactly where I needed to be and that is where He led me. I also did not want to force Carl to go with me since he was not a churchgoer, but he refused to send me off to church alone. That was God's plan too, for He was about to perform yet another miracle. He not only redeemed my life from the pit, He was about to save Carl's life through the gift of salvation.

Dear Derrick,

What a sea of despair I have been in without you! My tears have been my food day and night. Do you know just how much I miss you my son? The thought of living without you is more than I can bear. I thought it was supposed to get better with time. On the contrary, I feel as if I'm drowning—drowning in my very own sea of sorrow. My friends and family think I am doing okay, and believe me I am trying. Some days I can hold it together—other days the smallest thing provokes the pain inside of me and I fall apart. It comes without warning too, and there is nothing I can do to stop it. I feel so powerless. It may be a sad song on the radio, or watching a garbage truck go by, or eating a piece of cantaloupe or pineapple. They remind me of you and suddenly I am over-whelmed with emotion—mainly sorrow, because I miss you so terribly much. It just seems so in-credibly unfair that you had to die at such a young age. You never got a chance at life. You were never able to see the Statue of Liberty like you wanted. There are just so many 'nevers.' You will never graduate from high school; never have a girl-friend; never go to college; never get married; and, never have children. Not only are you denied these things, so am I. I will never watch you earn your diploma, or see you walk down the aisle, or hold your baby in my arms. I grieve for both of us, Derrick. My tears are for the experiences that you and I will never have together.

I have to tell you, though, that God did an amazing thing. He visited me in my dreams. I know it was Him, and He gave me a revelation of the future. I was drowning in a sea of sorrow, and He rescued me from my enemy who was too power-ful for me. Not once, but twice. And then He put my feet on spacious ground. In a way that I could innately understand, He revealed to me that I would be okay. He literally descended into the pit with me, and He lifted me up out of the mud and mire and rescued me. I know it will not be easy to go on without you and I may even have some set-backs, but I know He is for me, not against me, and He will not let the enemy destroy me through your death. I think He has bigger plans for me, little one. His plans for you were fulfilled in such a short amount of time and then you were ushered into His holy presence. His plans for me are to leave me here for the time being, yet I do believe that He will comfort and heal my broken heart. I have to let Him, because if I don't I am merely surviving, not living, and I know that you would want me to live. If nothing else, I must live for the both of us.

I will experience things down here for the both of us Derrick, okay? I want to feel laughter and joy again. Please understand that when I do, it will not lessen my love for you one bit. Neither will it mean that I no longer miss you, because I will never stop missing you. But I need to breathe life again—real life. Not just death. And I know that in some spiritual way you and I will remain connected for a part of you will always be living in and with me.

Love, Your Mom

Have you come to the Red Sea
place in your life,
Where, in spite of all you can do,
There is no way out, there is no way back,
There is no other way but through?
Then wait on the Lord with a trust serene
Till the night of your fear is gone;
He will send the wind, He will heap
the floods,
When He says to your soul, "Go on."
And His hand will lead you through—
clear through—
Ere the watery walls roll down,
No foe can reach you, no wave can touch,
No mightiest sea can drown;
The tossing billows may rear their crests,
Their foam at your feet may break,
But over their bed you shall walk dry shod
In the path that your Lord will make.
In the morning watch, 'neath the
lifted cloud,
You shall see but the Lord alone,
When He leads you on from the place
of the sea
To a land that you have not known;
And your fears shall pass as your foes
have passed,
You shall be no more afraid;
You shall sing His praise in a better place,
A place that His hand has made.

Annie Johnson Flint

"Fear not, for I have redeemed you; I have summoned you by name; you are mine. When you pass through the waters, I will be with you; and when you pass through the rivers, they will not sweep over you. When you walk through the fire, you will not be burned; the flames will not set you ablaze. For I am the Lord, your God, the Holy One of Israel, your Savior."   *Isaiah 43: 1-3*

Even though God gave me the vision of a redeemed life, He demanded my participation. I would not get well just by wishing it or expecting God to miraculously take the pain away. It hurts so deeply to lose a child through death—it always has, and no doubt, always will. I have always believed that with the same magnitude and depth of love that we feel for someone, we hurt when they are taken from us. This explained why it hurt so much to lose Derrick. It hurt so much because I loved him so much.

I also recognized that I had to be an active participant in bringing about my healing. At times I felt like I was taking one step forward and two steps back. There were no more dreams, no more miraculous signs or divine interventions. How I wished I could hear from God audibly or see into the distant future that everything would work out.

But then it wouldn't be faith, would it? God's Word says, *"Now faith is being sure of what we hope for and certain of what we do not see" (Hebrews 11:1).* If I could see it, it would not be faith. I must believe it. I must believe Him. I must believe in myself. I must believe in His power and ability to take all the broken pieces and put me back together again—kind of like 'Humpty Dumpty.'

When Derrick died, I lost my balance and fell backwards. I descended into a deep pit and shattered into a thousand, tiny pieces. It would be ludicrous to think that in my own strength I could pull myself out of this bottomless pit to put myself back together again. Never. Only Omnipotent God could do that. And I found out that that is precisely His specialty. Choosing the weak things of the world to shame the strong. Using the lowly and despised things to call us unto Himself. God's Word states, *"My grace is sufficient for you, for my power is made perfect in your weakness" (2 Corinthians 12:9).* That must mean that He is able to take the broken pieces and put them back together again even stronger and better than before.

And that is exactly what He did. Day by day, piece by piece, He masterfully began His work in me. I think it all started when He made me aware of how broken I really was without Him. Not only physically and emotionally—but especially spiritually. Regrettably in my past, I turned to people and things to make me happy. I had many 'voids' in my life, but tried to fill these voids with others and through materialism. Instead of looking at loneliness as an opportunity to delve into myself to ask and pursue the answers to the deeper questions of life, I associated loneliness with unhappiness. I thought every moment of every day had to be fun, exciting, packed with adventure, and, of course, filled with people—lots of people. After all, that is the true measure of your worth, right? Is it any wonder that I turned to people first with my deep sorrow expecting them to take it all away? To my dismay, I found out that people only disappointed me. Not intentionally, but then again, they are not supposed to be our savior—there is only one Savior and that is Jesus Christ. So why did it take me so long to recognize that mere mortals were incapable of filling any void in my life?

It was only after suffering such a devastating loss that my eyes began to slowly open to so many truths. Truth about who God is and what He alone can do. Although it may have been hurtful and yet another blow to realize that others will only let me down, in reality, it was God's gift to me. It allowed me, for the first time ever, to fully turn to Him. My tears were solely directed to Him as I began to turn over every ounce of sorrow and pain, expecting nothing of anyone else, and yet expecting everything of God.

I recall my dream when God reached down from on high and rescued me from my enemy and from drowning in a sea of sorrow and despair. He set my feet on dry land. I remember being alone in this spacious and vast wilderness that stretched out for miles in front of me. Yet I knew that I was not really alone—we would be journeying together from now on. He had a lot to teach me in these wilderness wanderings.

Just as Moses wandered in the desert for forty years, God was with him constantly providing, teaching, and guiding. I no longer felt utterly hopeless as I did in the pit, but in this wilderness I still felt pain. The tormenting anguish left me only to be replaced with a tender, yet deep-feeling ache in the very marrow of my bones. I became painfully aware of my own sinfulness, and the reality of who I had become was disheartening. The numerous sins of my past haunted me. How did I ever get to this point? How could I have been so selfish and sinful all at the same time? Although tears were my constant companions, I knew that I was not alone—God was with me in these wilderness wanderings, and this is where He began His greatest work in my life. Yes, the pain of losing Derrick was still so real, but now I had been given hope for my future. Somehow I had to be resurrected from this mess that I had become. The 'furnace of affliction' would be the tool God would use to purify me.

It was in the wilderness, while still in the furnace of affliction, that I began my new journey with Jesus. My sins were ever before me and no longer confined to my head, they had penetrated their way deep into my heart. It pained me to think of the person that I had become. I was selfish, self-reliant, and very hedonistic. All I cared about was me—what concerned me and what made me happy. No longer could I excuse my actions on immaturity. Simply put, I was living without God, and in many ways had even become my own god. Although I had always believed in a Supreme God, I did not know Him personally. I prayed on occasion or when I needed something from Him, but that was the extent of my Christianity. I basically lived my life in my own strength in the manner that I so chose. It did not matter to me one bit what others thought or said, including my own family.

I am ashamed to admit that I was a carnal Christian to say the least, sinful down to the very core of my being. God's Spirit awakened me to this very sad reality, and with deep-felt sorrow I confessed all of my sins to Him. I asked for forgiveness for all the immoral choices I had made and asked God to rectify my past. Even though many of my sins and sinful choices hurt others, especially my own family, I prayed that God would in some miraculous way make up for all the wrong I had done. I know He heard and forgave me, and it was sweet relief to come clean before Him. Little did I know that all my sins were burdens and weights that I was unnecessarily carrying. In some erroneous way I believed that God was punishing me because of them. Although my older sister,

Rosi, had always told me that God does not work that way, I could not quite convince myself of that until I heard God whisper His forgiveness into my heart. And no, He did not take my son to punish me for my sins. I was so relieved to know that.

I rededicated my life to Christ and vowed to make Him an integral part of it. An occasional quick prayer here and there no longer satisfied. I longed for answers to deeper questions. I wanted a meaningful and significant relationship with Jesus. God placed in my heart a desire to seek after Him and experience Him intimately. I was filled with questions that no one else could answer. How could this tragedy have occurred? Why did God allow it in the first place? I know He could have stopped it from happening. Why am I here? What is my purpose in this life? All of a sudden nothing else could satisfy that deep yearning that God put into my heart. I understood that the past was history, and no amount of prayer or faith would bring Derrick back to me. He would not mysteriously rise from the dead as Lazarus did. While in this furnace of affliction, I slowly began to see glimmers of hope again. This hope enabled me to put one foot in front of the other, one day at a time. It was as if God gave me just enough light for the step in front of me. No more, no less. It must have been His way to teach me to trust Him. Trust Him for today, and then trust Him again for tomorrow.

I was in this furnace of affliction in these wilderness wanderings for what seemed like an eternity. At times it became unbearable and I just wanted to escape it all again—kind of like the Israelites who grumbled and asked to go back to Egypt even after God rescued them from bondage, parted the Red Sea, and brought them into the desert on their way to the promised land. Those were the times when I turned back to drinking, or expected a friend or loved one to understand exactly how I felt and to somehow make me feel better. Unfortunately, these were once again idle attempts to fix things 'my way' instead of God's way. Through God's grace I have learned that with grief and suffering there are no 'quick fixes.' It takes lots of time, lots of tears, and lots and lots of God.

In the Bible it says that trials are like a refining process that burns away impurities and prepares us to meet Christ. Just as it takes intense heat to purify gold and silver by allowing the impurities to float to the top and be skimmed off, it often takes the heat of trials for a Christian to be purified. These very trials teach us patience and help us grow into the kind of people that God wants. I obviously had a lot of growing to do— otherwise I would not have had to stay in this furnace for so long. One thing I can say—God taught me valuable lessons in this 'school of suffering.' He taught me things that I know I would not have learned on easy street. He taught me about perseverance, and He breathed new hope and life into me, all the while transforming my character and purifying my heart. He refined me through the pain of losing Derrick in a way that I believe nothing else would have.

Sure, it is easy to complain when life becomes difficult. You ask yourself many questions like why would a loving God allow unpleasant experiences to come to His children? Sometimes God does test us in the furnace of affliction. I have also learned that instead of complaining, which renders no positive result, I absolutely must run to Him in faith for the strength to endure. As I do, my faith in Him grows exponentially and it actually gets easier to trust Him. I think faith is like a spiritual muscle. At first it is so very difficult to let go and let God, just like it is difficult to lift weights for the first time. However, the more you exercise your muscles, the easier it becomes to lift the weight. Likewise, the more you give your burdens, sorrows, and pain over to God and see Him at work in your life, the more your faith grows. Your 'spiritual muscles' have been strengthened.

God's Word breathed truth into my soul. His Word was a healing balm for my wounded heart. The stories in the Bible came to life and seemed to parallel mine in significant ways. One such story occurred in Exodus. When Moses and the Israelites were rescued by God, it was God Himself who parted the waters and they went through the sea on dry ground to escape the Egyptians. After this mighty deliverance and while still in their desert wanderings, the entire community grumbled and complained for lack of food and drink. So what did God do? He rained down manna from heaven. This manna was 'heavenly bread' and nothing like the Israelites had ever seen or tasted before. It was white and flaky in appearance and needed to be ground like grain and then boiled or baked. It also came in a most unusual way. Every morning there was a layer of dew around the camp. When the dew was gone, thin flakes like frost appeared on the ground. The Israelites were commanded to go and gather as much of the manna as they needed and were to fill a large container with this heavenly bread. The manna was a gift from God and it came every single day. The only day they were to gather two days' worth was on the sixth day because the next day was the Sabbath, and they were not to work on that day, but rest. Each Israelite gathered what he needed—some gathered much and some gathered little. Yet he who gathered little was just as satisfied as he who gathered and needed more. They were, however, commanded not to save any leftovers for as sure as they did, it would become maggot-infested.

The implication behind this story spoke volumes to me. God initially delivered the Israelites out of their enemies' hands because they were too strong for them. He parted the waters and put them on dry ground. Similarly, my enemy was too strong for me too, so God rescued me from the violent storm and put me on spacious, dry ground. Although the Israelites complained of hunger, in God's mercy He provided them with heavenly bread—manna. Their job was to go and collect it every single day. They needed to gather just enough for the day, no more and no less. If they gathered more or tried to hoard it, it would only go bad. He was asking them to trust Him to provide for their daily physical needs. Had the Israelites remained in their tents continuing to complain, and not doing anything to help themselves, they would have perished.

Jesus can be compared to manna—He is our daily bread who satisfies our eternal and spiritual needs. Had I continued to wallow in self-pity and despair when He was offering a way out through His grace, I would have perished in my own affliction. His daily manna was the portion of grace I needed to make it through that day, not tomorrow, or next week, but only for today. The days I failed to collect the manna (or grace) He had waiting for me are the days I felt especially weak and vulnerable. Those are the times I backslid and did not think I could take one more step forward. The days when I paused to take my fill of the heavenly grace that He sent just for me are the days when I felt strong. Those are the times when I felt a greater force at work within me enabling me to do what I knew I could not do on my own. The bottom line is that God is ever-present, ready, willing, and able to help us in our time of need, but we need to join hands with His and take the grace He so freely offers. He sends us our daily portion, but will we come out of our tents to collect it?

What a great lesson God taught me through reading this Old Testament story!

Dear Derrick,

If you could see me now I think you'd be proud of me. As difficult as it is to continue living without you, God is giving me glimmers of hope. He is speaking to me in marvelous ways that I can clearly understand. The dream He previously gave me was so significant and initially gave me a vision for my future. Now I can hear Him whisper to my heart through His Spirit, His Word, in my thoughts, and in other intangible ways that are hard to describe. I know it is Him and in His power He is transforming me. Slowly, one day at a time, He is altering my outlook on life and death. I think He is giving me His perspective, and believe me, it is so much better than mine. Mine only sees the pain of today—His sees the glory of eternity.

I have started going back to church and the things I am learning are incredible. Stories I have known for a long time are coming to life. I joined a Bible study and am actively working with God through the sorrow to find deeper significance. He is purifying my heart and I am seeing my sins as I have never seen before and it sure is ugly. I am so incredibly sorry, Derrick, for all the wrong I have done. I should have been a better mother. I shouldn't have been so selfish and worried about my own comfort. Can you please forgive me? A good friend of mine once said, "When you know

154

better, you do better." At times I guess I just didn't know any better. I also know that I can't beat myself up over my mistakes either. The past is gone, and I've been forgiven by God through Jesus' blood. Now I must look ahead to the future and what God wants for me.

I know He is going to continue to change me from the inside out. It hurts, but at the same time He does it so tenderly. It means I have to die to myself—my old ways, and my selfishness. Ironically, at times I resist this change, but other times I welcome it. I know it is for my best. I also know that it is the only way. I cannot remain the same person I was. My life has been so drastically altered since the day you died and I need to become better. I need to grow spiritually—knowing about Him no longer satisfies. I need to **know** Him. God has planted a seed in my heart and one day it will bear fruit. Right now I just need to trust and seek after Him.

I wrote this poem several years after your death. God's Spirit was moving in my heart and I wanted to document everything I was feeling. What followed flowed so easily as if God Himself were speaking directly to me. The words brought me comfort and peace. I hope you like it.

Love, Your Mom

Derrick

A special little boy the Lord once gave to me
His brief life would be the tool God used to
set me free
Though his life on earth would be nine years
For him forever would cease all fears
For the Lord would spare this little soul
From suffering, pain, and growing old
But now His work was to begin on me
From my own ways it was time to flee
He patiently carried me day by day
And gave me strength so my soul wouldn't
wither away
For the pain stabbed my heart and the grief
was so deep
So often all I could do was weep
But I wasn't weeping alone I now know
For the Father's tears alongside mine did flow
He knew it was necessary for me like this
to feel
Before my soul could begin to heal
It didn't happen instantly or even overnight
But with time the Lord gave me the gift of
true sight
No, he wasn't trying to punish me
On the contrary, it was time to set me free
Set me free from worldliness and sin
And allow the change in me to begin
As I took time to be with Him
He revealed to me His light would never dim

He'd be with me forevermore
All that was required of me was to knock
on His door
When I knocked on His door, it opened wide
And with arms outstretched He welcomed
me inside
He didn't promise me a new life without pain
But in an instant a great Comforter and Friend
I did gain
He replaced my deep pain with peace and joy
All of this through my little boy
At last I know he did not die in vain
For his mother's soul will be his gain
I am so thankful that the Lord came after me
And that at last through His eyes I can see
See His great tenderness and love
Sent to every one of us from up above
So when you go through trials and pain
Remember the sun will replace the rain
Call on the Father who loves you so much
And let your soul feel His healing touch
He doesn't want you to go through it alone
He will be with you till He calls you home
At last you will see purpose in your sorrow
For today's pain and affliction will be forever
replaced in Heaven's tomorrow.

Walk to Emmaus

Now that same day two of them were going to a village called Emmaus, about seven miles from Jerusalem. They were talking with each other about everything that had happened. As they talked and discussed these things with each other, Jesus himself came up and walked along with them; but they were kept from recognizing him...When he was at the table with them He took bread, gave thanks, broke it and began to give it to them. Then their eyes were opened and they recognized him, and he disappeared from their sight. They asked each other, "Were not our hearts burning within us while he talked with us on the road and opened the Scriptures to us?" Luke 24:13-16, 30-32

It was March of 2000. Already ten years had passed since Derrick left his earthly existence. I was invited to attend a special retreat called the 'Walk to Emmaus.' I had often heard about this spiritual pilgrimage and now I was signed up to go. Not anyone can attend one of these special retreats. You actually have to be invited and sponsored by a past participant. This person must know you personally and believe that you are ready to receive, with an open heart, all God has in store for you.

It just boggles my mind how God some-times works. My sponsor came into my life in the form of a realtor. She sold us the home we were currently living in. Our paths crossed for a short while only. Could it be that we met not just for another house sale, but more specifically, so that I would attend the Walk to Emmaus? I have come to appreciate that with God there are no coinci-dences. In fact, coincidences are merely God's way of remaining anonymous. We must actively look for him in these so-called circumstances. Yes, I believe that she was brought into my life for a reason. I was to attend this special retreat. How God would manifest His holy presence to me through this four day pilgrimage would absolutely blow my mind!

The first amazing turn of events occurred before I even was aware of it. The retreat was scheduled to be held at a camp located on the out-skirts of town. For unknown reasons, the location of the retreat was changed at the last minute to Christ United Methodist Church in Middletown, Ohio. This change of venue really bothered me because Middletown, Ohio, had so many memories for me. Not only was Derrick born in this city, but this very church was the one that Derrick, Travis and I attended for awhile. It was also in this church that Carl and I were married. Although I have many wonderful memories of times in Middle-town, the thought of going back to this small town troubled me immensely. This place represented my old life, and this is the town I lived in when Derrick died. I had moved out of my house and out of this town a little over a year after Derrick died. My new home was twenty miles south in a suburb of Cincinnati, and I had absolutely no reason to visit Middletown ever again. The memories there were just too painful. Why on earth would this retreat be held in Middletown in the very same church I used to attend?

Reluctantly, I decided to go anyway. After all, I was already sponsored and they were expecting me. Some very wonderful things happened on these sacred grounds—things too numerous to even recall. All I can say is that I felt loved and embraced by countless people that I had never met before. I later learned that every moment of this long weekend was being covered in prayer and that each participant was prayed over. It was a 24-hour prayer vigil and we were prayed for by name by people we did not even know. The number of volunteers it took to pull off this event was incredible. Cooks, servers, and the myriad of behind the scenes volunteers were astonishing. It was their job to feed us, sing with us, lead us, and wholeheartedly pour out 'agape' love to us.

Upon arrival we were asked to put away all cell phones and watches. No outside communication of any kind was allowed. In fact, we were sort of 'locked up' the entire four days. There were many women attending this retreat, but it still felt very personal as we were divided into small groups. We did a variety of activities—we performed skits, sang songs, prayed, laughed, and cried together. We shared our stories with one another—painful ones I might add. One seemed to be worse than the next. How could there be such sorrow in a room filled with such wonderful women? The beautiful irony is we carried one another's burdens as we shared our deepest sorrows. Numerous times we were led into the chapel, praying, and sharing communion. The days were filled with countless speeches by our leaders as they covered a variety of topics, and yet we still had plenty of time to get to know each other in a very meaningful way. The amazing thing is we were completely open and vulnerable with one another. We shared our stories and our struggles.

At one point I felt led to share my story of the death of my son, and as I so often did, burst into tears. Instead of compassionate stares, they began crying with me. When it was our group's time to share with the rest of the participants, they decided not to do a funny skit as many other groups did, but instead shared my story of loss. Then we sang in unison one of the songs played at Derrick's funeral—"As the Deer Pants for Water" together. There was not a dry eye in the room. What a beautiful display of love they exhibited as they mourned my loss with me. For those brief moments, they shared the burden of my pain, and I could see in their eyes that they hurt too.

Each night as we returned to our beds little trinkets were left on our pillows. These were gifts of love made by people from all over. Among these gifts were bookmarks, poems, key chains, and potholders, just to name a few. Many were inscribed with Bible verses. We were given notes of encouragement and how they were praying for us.

One of the very special moments of the weekend was when all participants were given a large, oversized envelope. We were told to find a quiet place where we could open our envelopes. I quickly found a secluded spot and tore mine open. I found individual note cards and letters from people near and dear to me—letters from Carl, my sisters, my friends, and others who knew me well. Each letter or note card represented someone who took the time to write me a note of love and encouragement. I was touched as I read their words and I felt embraced, accepted, and loved. This was another one of those 'secret' things that my sponsor took care of weeks before the retreat. In fact, none of the participants knew anything about these special letters or the other meaningful activities that would take place. Imagine the things we shared as a group when we reunited after our tearful moments!

By far the most memorable experience for me occurred on the last day of the retreat. It was a Sunday afternoon and we were concluding the retreat by having a final church service. As we entered the sanctuary, I could see that other than a few empty rows left vacant for the participants, the entire place was filled with people. I was told that they were former participants of a Walk to Emmaus retreat. It may have been years since their own personal pilgrimage, but it was a standard practice to invite all former participants. The purpose of their attendance was to shower us with love and support.

As the current participants felt led, they approached the altar to share their weekend experience with those in the pews. This was not mandatory and not all participants shared. Before I knew it, I jumped to my feet and approached the altar. So many wonderful things happened to me over the course of these last four days that I felt compelled to share with the others. I cannot remember everything I said, but I allowed myself to be completely vulnerable as I shared my painful past with these total strangers. I told them about losing my precious 9 year old son in a tragic accident in this very city ten years ago. I did not give details as to how he died, but I completely opened my heart to them, and they felt my pain. Without any warning, my small group rose to their feet and made their way to where I was standing. They lovingly put their arms around me as I wept and struggled to speak. This gave me strength, and I proceeded to testify that I knew God was working in my life through my sorrow. I trusted Him and believed that He would work out all things for my good. He would continue to help me carry my heavy cross and one day use it for His glory.

As I looked into the faces of the crowd, my eyes met my sponsor's eyes. She was there too, and after the service she would drive me home. We had a twenty minute ride to my house, but she wanted to hear all about my weekend experience. We decided to stop at Perkins fifteen miles up the road to grab a bite to eat. I was filled with such excitement I could barely contain myself as I shared with her story after story. We ordered our food and as we began to eat, a man approached our table. He knelt down beside me and asked me if I had just been at Christ United Methodist Church in Middletown at the Walk to Emmaus retreat. I nodded my head and replied, "Yes, I just came from there a little while ago." He proceeded to tell me that he was there too and had just heard my story. He then asked me if my son by chance died in an elevator accident on Marymont Court. My heart began to beat faster and I answered, "Yes, he did." I had an instinctive feeling that what this man would utter next would be profound. It was.

He took my hand and told me that he was one of the firefighters called to the scene of the accident where my son had died. My heart almost burst out of my body as I began to cry and shake. I couldn't believe that this man kneeling here beside me was one of the last people to see my little boy. His eyes saw my son's crushed face and lifeless body for he was there to help retrieve Derrick's broken body out of that elevator closet. He wept with me, and then told me that a few years later he gave his life to Christ. I know that these incidents must deeply affect other people too. He, no doubt, experienced his very own nightmare by personally attending to a young, dead child with a marred face. Once again, I was thankful that I was not the one who saw my boy's disfigured face. God have mercy on this man who did.

This was another moment when God unmistakably revealed His manifest presence to me. This was indeed a divine appointment, a message sent directly from God. It was His incredible gift given to me—to be able to see and talk to the man who was there to free my son's body from the elevator. God wanted me to know how profoundly it affected him, and I also believe that God wanted to bring me closure. I asked the man if my son had suffered and what the cause of death was. Even though I had a death certificate signed by the county coroner that outlined the cause of death, it was something altogether different to hear it in person from someone who was on the scene. He told me that Derrick died of asphyxiation and that he did not suffer. The blow to the back of his head rendered him unconscious. I was thankful for his explanation. As horrific as the accident was, it was sweet relief to hear that Derrick did not suffer and feel pain. We said goodbye, he returned to his table, and my sponsor and I finished our meal.

What a divine encounter! Twenty miles from the church where the retreat was conducted, God made sure that our paths would cross, and that we would be able to share a few healing words with one another—as the mother of the deceased child and the firefighter who freed his body from the elevator. This brief divine encounter brought me so much comfort, and I hope it encouraged him too. Who knows, he may have often wondered what became of this child's mother? How did she cope with his death? Maybe it was also God's gift to him to personally meet me and see God's miraculous work in my life.

My sponsor and I drove the rest of the way to my home in silence. My mind was trying to comprehend everything that had just transpired. A few hundred yards from my house she abruptly stopped her car as we saw several deer feeding in a nearby yard. Oh, my goodness, another sign from God! I sat there in bewilderment as I watched these beautiful animals. You see, the presence of deer has had special significance to me for quite some time now. When God allows deer to cross my path, I immediately think of Him. They are my clear, visual reminder of His presence in my life. Once again, He confirmed His love and approval to me through their visit. At this point, I was on cloud nine and my spirit was overflowing with thanksgiving and praise to God.

As I entered my home to greet my family, I was so happy to be alive—so happy to be loved by them and above all by God. His mercy and favor rested on me that weekend and it is one that I will never forget. I truly encountered Jesus on my very own Walk to Emmaus. He met me in a special way, and there is no mistaking that I heard His inaudible voice to my spirit loud and clear. I felt His love through the love of complete strangers. I humbly accepted His unconditional forgiveness for all my sins. I experienced His mercy and grace, and I saw with my own eyes God's abundant love poured out just for me. He sees the pain I carry in my heart for He feels it too.

Yes, God revealed Himself in amazing ways on my pilgrimage. He confirmed to me that He had been journeying with me all along through my wilderness—there was never a time when I had been alone. Only now could I see it. Just like the two believers who left Jerusalem after the crucifixion on their way to Emmaus. At first they did not know that it was Jesus who joined them for they were very sad and preoccupied with the events that just occurred in Jerusalem. In the same manner, I had a spiritual awakening and there was no denying that something profound was happening deep within my spirit. I think God had been trying to communicate with me all along, but far too often I was too focused on my pain and disappointments to see or hear Him clearly. Though a slow student in this school of suffering, I began to learn that when I looked for Jesus in my midst, that is when I began to experience His power and help. Although

I believed God's Word that He never leaves nor forsakes us, it was as if the veil had been lifted from my eyes, and now I could see things formerly invisible and hear things formerly inaudible. The God of heaven and earth was communicating with me for He longed to bring me peace and healing. I knew with full certainty that I was experiencing God's power and love beyond my wildest expectations and that I was not walking alone. Jesus was with me all along.

Dear Derrick,

Many years have passed since my eyes last beheld your beautiful, little face. I wish so much I could hold your hands and look into your big, blue eyes again. I must tell you though that my vision is beginning to change. Things are becoming much clearer to me almost as if I am now wearing the correct lenses for the first time. My vision is changing from a temporal view to an eternal one. I am beginning to see things I could not see before. It's as if God has lifted a heavy veil from my eyes and is giving me His eternal vision. I may not be able to tangibly see you, but I can see you with God's eyes. I can see you with Jesus and I know you are happy. You know what, Derrick? I am happy too.

I can't even begin to tell you all the amazing things that Jesus is doing for me. He is going out of His way to reveal Himself to me in big ways that I simply can't miss.

Proverbs 29:18 says, "Where there is no vision, the people perish." I will not perish for God is giving me a new vision for my life. There truly has been purpose in my pain and suffering. God has been slowly chipping away the old and making me new. I know He is all about character transformation, and boy is He doing a number on me. You may not even recognize me anymore! I am changing from the inside out and my heart is mending. Slowly, day by day, His love and grace are making me whole again. I know you would be happy to know that. Your brief life on earth has completely transformed mine.

Do you know what a gift you have been to me? I know for certain that I would not be who I am today had you not been my son. God is continually working and bringing me a peace that truly surpasses understanding. I miss you terribly, but I am grieving differently now. I am finally grieving with hope—hope for tomorrow, but mostly hope for eternity. I know our eyes will meet again, and I look forward to that day. In the meantime, I will live and learn all that I can down here in this brief life that God has given me.

I can see Jesus clearly now through the suffering, and God is giving me a new passion and purpose for life. It involves you. We will be forever connected for my purpose in living is to tell others about you through my story, and the incredible love, mercy, and grace of God, my Father.

Love, Your Mom

Lessons Learned   18

"Call to me and I will answer you and tell you great and unsearchable things you do not know."   *Jeremiah 33:3*

I always hated the old cliché 'Time Heals Wounds.' What a terrible thing to say to someone who has just lost a loved one. It implies that with time you will get over it—you will not hurt anymore nor will you cry any longer. In fact, it almost insinuates that you will simply forget your loved one, hence no more tears or pain. Nothing is farther from the truth. It has been almost twenty years since my son died at that birthday party, and I have not forgotten him. On the contrary, I think of him daily. My mind wonders all the time—what would he have looked like now? What career path would he have chosen? Would he be married and have children? The list goes on and on. Some days the pain is just as vivid as on the day he died. Of course, no one can visibly see what I still feel in my heart. Maybe I should be 'over it' by now. After all, it has been so many years since Derrick died. In looking back over my own experience of grief, I have come to accept that as a parent you never get 'over it.' You get through it, and you do not get through it alone either.

The absolute hardest ingredient in suffering is time. What time did is allow me to come to the end of myself, show me the depths of my own depravity, and lead me to the only one, Jesus, who could heal my broken heart. Believe me—I tried everything else I could in an attempt to take away the immense pain; however, nothing worked. I found out that you never know that Jesus is all you need until Jesus is truly all you've got. He is the one who transformed me and gave me His perspective. I must state though that He did use time—His time, because He knew that I could not take in all He had to give me at once. So a little here, a little there, He began to perform His mastery in me.

One of the greatest things God did was point out my own inadequacy. In His mercy, He allowed me to come to the cold, hard realization that the only way I would survive this devastating loss was to set my mind on eternal things. I could no longer live for the here and now because it had the power to destroy me. After all, there was nothing else to live for. My son was dead and he was not coming back. I realized that I was a desperate case, and that I needed divine intervention from God. Indeed, it would take a miracle to change my outlook and heal my broken heart, but I found out that is just up God's alley.

If life were summed up as only a temporary existence wherein we lived for a short time, sought after happiness, prosperity, and pleasure, and then returned as dust to the earth, then I so agree with

King Solomon—life is truly meaningless. I wanted no part of that philosophy. God taught me that only in Him does life have meaning and true pleasure. Furthermore, this doesn't mean that we are exempt from hardships and difficulties—rather we learn and grow through them. We need to remind ourselves that God's grace is truly sufficient for us. Human weakness provides the ideal opportunity for the display of divine power. Well, I sure needed His divine power because in my own strength I was totally incapable of picking up the pieces to go on. It wasn't a one time decision either. Every morning when I awoke, my nightmare would begin all over again. Then I'd cry out to God once again and ask for His presence and strength. This happened day after day, week after week, for a long, long time.

Even now—almost twenty years later, I could so easily succumb and fall into the pit of despair. There are days when I return to that dark cave and in some strange sort of way even find comfort there for a short while. The pain returns with fervency and I feel the deep anguish of my soul. I remember where I was and how utterly desperate and alone I felt. There in my solitude, I cry over the loss of my son for I still miss him so terribly much. Yet I am reminded of God's grace and love to me in the midst of such sorrow. God allows me to experience the sorrow, but I no longer linger there. After a brief while, He lifts me up again and restores my soul. He fills me anew with his sufficient grace and reminds me of my eternal home. He whispers to my heart, *"In this world you will have trouble my child, but take heart! I have overcome the world" (John 16:33).* I sincerely believe Him.

Whoever said life was going to be easy? Sometimes it is downright difficult and every breath we take hurts so deeply. There is so much injustice, pain and suffering in this world, but I have learned that God does something absolutely amazing through all of our heartaches. He performs radical surgery of the heart if we but trust in Him even when we can't see the step in front of us. He does bind up our wounds and heal them. However, they do leave a scar. Just as Jesus had scars on His hands and feet to represent the price He paid to secure our eternal salvation, we have our own battle scars. Although they may all look different, they are our reminders of a gracious God who loved us too much to leave us broken and separated from Him. He's shown me that adversity in whatever form it may take is His way of drawing mankind back to Him. Mine just happened to be through my little boy. Some scars are bigger and deeper than others, and all who see them are aware of the intense battle that took place for the wounds to be so deep. Behind these deep wounds is the great Physician and Healer who painstakingly touches the broken pieces of our souls and in His way, in His time, and in His strength allows the wound to slowly heal. God knows that our greatest victories come from apparent defeats. And though Satan's sole desire is to destroy us and he fights viciously for our souls, no one can snatch God's little ones out of His hands.

Another life-saving lesson God taught me in my wilderness wanderings was that my greatest ambition in life was to know Him. To do this would require me to diligently seek after Him with all my heart. My journey to know God began so slowly and quite simply—a little devotional here, a Christian book there. I thank God for all the wonderful authors who boldly profess His name and help those of us who are struggling to find the answers. The only thing that really mattered to God was that I come—just as I am. God would do the rest. I just had to show up for my appointment with Him. To the outside world these may have all appeared to be tiny steps, but they were huge steps to God. He used them to draw me to a deeper revelation and awareness of Him.

I made an interesting discovery—the days when I neglected Him were the very days that I had a difficult time dealing with life's hard blows. The days I sought Him, tears and all, were the days when I was lifted higher. I began to witness glimmers of hope and could even slightly detect a rainbow in the sky. I could laugh through my tears at funny stories about my boy, and I would forget, however momentarily, the pain of losing him. I would remember wonderful things about Derrick and the joy he brought to my life. These vivid memories would stir up anticipation of seeing him again one day. These glimpses filled me with hope, stretched my faith, and become pivotal in my moving forward for I did not want to rest content in the dark valley when I could see a glimpse of the summit awaiting me. God literally gave me a 'holy discontent' to spur me onward. I simply had to move forward. I could not continue to live my life as in a dark coal mine where no light could penetrate. I had to move forward and allow the sun to shine on my face once again. God showed me that it was time to leave behind the dark dungeon, that deep valley of sorrow, to begin my slow ascent up the mountain. He assured me that He would be there with me, picking me up when I would fall, and together we would climb one step at a time. I knew it would be a slow and arduous journey, but it consoled me knowing that I was not walking alone. He was beside me tenderly comforting and encouraging me. He was behind me giving me the courage to take yet another step when I was too weary. He was ahead of me cheering me onward and showing me the way to go.

As my heart became sensitive to His soft voice, I knew that I must make Him the source and center of my life in order to be able to fulfill the purpose He had for me. Yes, it was time to begin the upward climb to a higher place, a better place, and a fuller life. I would no longer linger in the lowlands simply because I was afraid to climb the giant mountain. Although the road was steep and rugged and to ascend it would take every ounce of strength I had, I was unexplainably drawn to the mountain heights. There just had to be something beautiful to behold once I reached the mountain peaks. Maybe the fresh mountain air would breathe new life into my weary soul, or maybe the warmth of the sun on my face would dry my constant stream of tears. Or maybe, just maybe, I would be able to encounter the glory of the Lord as Moses did in the burning bush and be able to see something wonderful beyond my pain. Whatever awaited me had to be better than wasting away in the dark mists of the sunless valley. Yes, onward I will climb.

Dear Jesus,

Please give me the courage for the mountain climb and be ever-present for I know that without you I cannot reach its heights. You tell us that your ways are higher than our ways and though I don't understand why all of this happened and why I am here in this deep valley, I so desperately need your help to climb out of it to begin my ascent toward the mountain summit.

Please lead me gently into the land of promise and let me not take one step beyond what my foot is able to endure. When I am so weary and weak and do not think I can take another step, strengthen me through your power and love. I will not give up for though my eyes cannot visibly see

you, my spirit feels your presence.   Together we
will make the climb one step at a time.
Love, your daughter Diana

Derrick drew this picture of Jesus on a cross when
he was just 4 years old.

"I tell you the truth, if you have faith as small as a mustard seed, you can say to this mountain, 'Move from here to there' and it will move. Nothing will be impossible for you."

Matthew 17:20-21

When we face hardship and discouragement it is easy to lose sight of the big picture. Fortunately, I have seen and heard so many stories of people who have already made it through life enduring far more difficult circumstances than I have experienced. The Bible shows us that suffering is the training ground for Christian maturity. It develops our patience and makes our final victory sweet. Likewise, I can honestly say without a shadow of a doubt, that not one thing in my life has had the power to influence or shape my life like suffering has.

Happy times have made me grateful, but haven't changed me. Fond memories have brought a smile to my heart, but haven't changed me. Great health has enabled me to live a relatively pain-free life, but hasn't changed me. Prosperity has given me the added blessing of living comfortably in nice surroundings, but it also hasn't changed me. On the contrary, deep suffering is the only experience that I can attribute to completely, irreversibly and intrinsically changing my entire being. It has changed my outlook on life and above all, my vision and purpose for living. It has challenged my faith to the core, transformed my character from the inside out, and reversed my entire vision and purpose for life. It has given me a hope that surpasses all understanding in a God who is good, a God who loves me immeasurably more than I can ever begin to fathom, and a compassionate God who will one day wipe away that last tear.

Yes, suffering has done its number on me. Needless to say, it took a great deal of time before I could even begin to see any good that could come from such suffering. It was not until I could take my eyes off of my circumstances and my unhappy state of being and look to God for answers that I began to catch any glimmer of hope. What made it so difficult was that I needed answers to questions that I simply did not have the capacity to understand. Believe me, I did question God, "Why? Why did Derrick have to die so young?" I wasted so much time doubting and wondering if God was even able to help me. Seriously, how on earth can anyone help another whose outcome is irreversible? Whose heart is broken and whose future looks so grim? No kind words can take away the constant stab in your heart. No amount of hugs or well wishes can bring about healing. And that is just the answer I was looking for—yet no one on earth could do that. It would take the mighty power of the God who created all of heaven and all of earth to minister to me personally.

It all started with the faith as small as a mustard seed that God implanted deep into my heart many years ago. Although planted, it remained stagnant and unable to grow due to the infertile soil of my heart. Immense tragedy turned up the hard soil and my mustard seed faith began to grow as it took root in Jesus. I got to the point where I knew it was Him or nothing else. Either Jesus would be able to reveal Himself to me in a way that I could understand or it would be slow, certain death. Eventually some of those 'why' questions no longer tormented me. I would find myself asking, "Why not me? What makes me so different from everyone else? Who says that I should be able to avoid any suffering?" Everyone who has a pulse has a cross to bear. Their cross may just look a little different than mine. Given enough time, we will all experience pain, suffering and loss. God help us that when tragedy does strike, we do have faith—even if it is as small as a mustard seed. God will use that little faith and multiply it in ways beyond our wildest expectations.

Faith was the hand of God that rescued me from the sea of pain I was drowning in. Faith was the weapon that destroyed my powerful enemies— doubt, discouragement, and despair, who confronted me in the day of my disaster. Faith was the shield of God that protected and kept me safe day after day. Faith was the powerful magnet that drew me to Him for hope and healing. Faith was the eagle's wings that have allowed me to soar high above my earthly circumstances and limited view to see clearly the face of Jesus. And faith will one day bring me home.

Yes, faith is truly being sure of what you hope for and certain of what you do not see. And *"without faith it is impossible to please God, because anyone who comes to Him must believe that He exists and rewards those who earnestly seek him" (Hebrews 11:6).* Every step I took in the direction of seeking God was a step of faith. I did not know how, when or where deliverance would come, but I did know that I had to believe in something bigger than myself or my pitiful circumstances. Why not God? I had a lot of questions for Him anyway. Although I knew about Him from stories I had heard over the years, I did not know Him personally. So what better time than now? My whole world just crumbled apart in a day, what else did I have to look forward to?

That tiny step of faith was crucial and all it took for God to begin to move in big ways. Believe me when I say tiny, I mean microscopic. The eyes of Omnipotent God saw my feeble efforts and when I took one small step, He took ten giant ones toward me. He planted in me the desire to seek after Him. I began finding myself drawn to Christian bookstores to browse through their books on grief. I'd look for material that would be palatable for me because at that time the Bible was just an overwhelmingly, hard-to-understand, history book. So He met me in the bookstore, and He met me in the pages of a devotional, or in a book about another parent's journey of grief. I became quite aware of the fact that I was not the only parent who had ever lost a child and was hurting. In addition, I could sense that God was grieving with me. It dawned on me that He Himself gave up His only Son for all mankind. Could it be possible that God knew exactly how I was feeling, and loved me anyway through all my doubts and discouragement? I felt His presence when I took the time to be with Him, and I liked how that felt. How pitiful I must have looked continually crawling to Him with an endless flow of tears streaming down my face. He understood and His only desire was to bring healing to my broken soul.

I am happy to report that eventually I did sign up for Bible study classes and opened the 'Big Book.' What an incredibly, life-changing, amazing book! All of a sudden it was not quite as overwhelming to me. It was as if God was preparing me all along so that He could reveal deeper truths to my heart. I began to find the Bible intriguing and the words written therein gently invoked a quiet and peaceful rest to my weary soul. I simply had no idea of the transforming power of God's written Word. Although it took many years for me to even desire to read it, the days I took the time to sit down and open God's Word were huge steps in the right direction—in God's direction. God's Word is truly life-changing. It gave me clear direction and guidance and comforted me beyond anything else I had previously tried. What took place between God, His Word, and me is nothing short of miraculous. Words cannot adequately describe what transpired between our spirits. I can shout from the rooftops that God's written Word is the primary tool He used to speak to me. Without a doubt, it is the single thing most directly responsible for the healing of my broken heart. It is also the secret key to my wonderful relationship with Him. I have found a true friend in Jesus—one who understands me and loves me anyway. One who continually beckons me to draw closer to Him for He alone can offer me living water and breathe new life into my spirit. Yes, faith as small as a mustard seed enabled me to open its beautiful pages, and God's Word is the truth that set me free.

One day not too long ago, I was reading a story in the Bible about the woman who had been plagued by profuse bleeding for over twelve years. She had suffered much and no doctor could heal her. In fact, under their care, she got worse. Then she heard about Jesus. He came to her town and she thought to herself if she could only touch his clothes she would be healed. She made her way through the crowds to touch his garment, and instantly her bleeding stopped and she was healed. Jesus, knowing who it was, asked the crowd, *"Who touched my clothes?"* She came and fell at His feet, trembling with fear, and told Him the entire truth and how she had been plagued with this illness. He turned to her and said, *"Daughter, your faith has healed you. Go in peace" (Luke 8:48).* As I read these words, God's Holy Spirit imparted truth to my spirit as He whispered to me, "Diana, your faith has healed you too."

Dear Derrick,

Can you see me from heaven, Derrick? Can you see what God is doing in my heart? If so, then surely you must be pleased. God is showing me the truth in His Word about life and its purpose and mostly, He is teaching me about Jesus and His amazing love. God's Word is so incredibly marvelous and powerful and healing all at the same time. But I don't need to tell you all of this because you already know. Oh, how I miss you. Please know that I will never forget you. Even though it has been so long since I've seen you, no amount of time will ever erase the wonderful memories I have stored of you in my heart. God has brought such healing to my soul, but that does not make me miss you any less. In fact, at times I miss you even more. I long to touch you and hold you close once again. I long to experience what you are experiencing and see Jesus as you do. I know that not a moment too soon will God usher me into His presence.

I am changing inside—I can feel it. Kind of like a butterfly ready to burst forth from its cocoon.

I am breaking free from the prison I have been in, and it is time to spread my wings and fly. God's Word is so encouraging and it breathes life into my very soul. It is truly a lamp unto my feet and a light unto my path (Psalm 119:105). Oh, yes, I still stumble and fall, but I know the One who gently picks me up and gives me the strength to walk again. You know I've always believed in Jesus, but I didn't know Him personally and intimately like I do now. Please forgive me for not telling you more about Him. I passed on to you the little I did know from my own childhood, but it was so insufficient. I am sorry I did not take the time to teach you more about Jesus and heaven. But then again, you knew more than I did, even at your young age.

Remember all those birthday and Mother's Day cards you made me? You always made sure to draw a picture of Jesus or the cross on them. I still carry in my Bible a bookmark you made for me. It says, "God Loves You," and has a picture of the cross on it. You even draped a veil over the cross and Jesus' blood was at the foot of the cross. I remember thinking how sweet of you to think of Jesus so much. Now I do too!

You knew in your short years what it has taken me a half a century to figure out. The faith of a little child is so precious in His sight. I am seeing with eyes of faith now too, and that is the only reason I can go on living without you. It has taken me awhile, but Jesus is so faithful and patient. He has rewarded my 'mustard seed' faith and multiplied it in unimaginable ways. I am reaching out to others who are hurting too with the same loss and pain as I experienced with you. I understand them because I feel their pain also. All I can do is encourage them to have faith as small as a mustard seed in a God who remains faithful and will work all things for good for those who love Him.

So my little one, I am okay here. I am doing the job God has given me to do and one day we will be together again. I promise.

Love, Your Mom

This picture was on an Easter card Derrick gave me when he was 7 years old.

Derrick made this card when he was 7 years old.

"Whenever I bring clouds over the earth and the rainbow appears in the clouds, I will remember my covenant between me and you and all living creatures of every kind. Never again will the waters become a flood to destroy all life. Whenever the rainbow appears in the clouds, I will see it and remember the everlasting covenant between God and all living creatures of every kind on the earth."   *Genesis 9:14-16*

September 21, 2009. Today would have been Derrick's 29th birthday. Ironically, he would now be the exact age I was when he died almost twenty years ago. It is hard to fathom that so many years have already passed. I miss him as much now as I did then. Actually, even more. I can't stop wondering what he would have been like. No doubt he would have been tall, handsome, but most of all, he would have been extremely kind. There was a sweet spirit in that child, and I'm sure it would have still been there even as an adult. He may have been married and possibly even had a few children of his own by now. However, that was not God's will for his life. After almost twenty years, I can honestly say that I have come to grips with that realization. Derrick's life, as brief as it was, was complete. He was a special child who accomplished everything that God intended for him to do.

The transformation God did in me, however long it seemed to take, was nothing short of a miracle. He lifted the veil of sorrow and gave me a new purpose for my life. I wish I could say it came quickly and easily. It did not. What I do know is that Jesus was with me every step of the way— even when feelings dictated otherwise. He comforted me, cried with me, prayed for me, encouraged me, and brought many special people into my life to love me even when I was quite unlovable. You see, grief takes its toll on a person. It is a long, slow, arduous journey full of twists and turns. Sometimes we need the hug of a friend or loved one to help us along. Sometimes we just need to be left alone.

What I have learned over the years is that grieving is truly a solitary journey. As much as we would like others to accompany us on our difficult path, we must go alone. Just as an eagle is a solitary bird that never flies in flocks, we, too, must walk through the valley of the shadow of death alone. The ironic thing is we really are not walking alone because God is walking with us. He is for us and will do all He can to heal us. He does require our participation though. We must be proactive in helping ourselves, and it is imperative that we do our part. God isolated me and drew me to Himself for only He could heal my broken heart. No kind words or well-meaning intentions could take away the deep pain I continued to experience in my soul. Jesus did heal my wounds, but He also left a scar. That scar is with me every single day and reminds me of His goodness, mercy, and incredible grace.

Jesus also had scars and when I look at them I am filled with love and gratitude to a God who loved me so much that He would send His Son to die for me. Before I was even born He knew my name, and He foresaw the cross I would bear. He knew that it would be heavy. Just as God was glorified and brought many sons to Him through the death of His Son, Jesus, He would be glorified again in my life through the death of my own son. Not only did he rescue and deliver me, He put a new song in my mouth and indescribable joy in my heart. He filled my heart with a desire for Him. If I don't praise Him and tell of His mighty works then the rocks will literally cry out. I cannot be silent. I must share my story for it truly is a story of hope and healing in the midst of great suffering and loss.

Today I relish every opportunity that God gives me to bring Him glory through my testimony for He has filled my heart with a joy and peace that surpasses understanding. My prayer is that those who read this book will be encouraged and realize that no matter what circumstances you may face in this life, God loves you with an indescribable love. He delights in you and He sings over you. He desires nothing more than for you to come to Him and build an intimate relationship with Him. Once you do, you cannot help but love Him, for He is a good God—all of the time. In addition, he promises to never leave or forsake you. On the contrary, He uses the painful experiences to bring you closer to Himself where He wants you to continually experience the joy of an abiding relationship with Him. Yes, you can have joy amidst the most painful times because joy is different than happiness. It flows much deeper and is a gift directly from God Himself.

I have also learned that there is no limit to the abundant blessings God wants to bestow on His children. Since the death of Derrick, God has blessed me with two other children, a son named Christopher, and a daughter named Erika. They did not, nor will they ever, take the place of Derrick. Nor are they supposed to. They are unique and beautiful individuals just as Derrick was. They are reminders to me of how gracious God is. They were springs of refreshment in my wilderness wanderings. They were gifts of hope for my weary journey. Yes, God knows just what we need when we need it. He gives, and sometimes He takes away.

In reflecting back over the years of my journey through the valley of pain and suffering, I can see His hand ever-present in my life. There were many times I did not think I would make it. Even though I wanted to give up on myself, God never gave up on me. He knew exactly when and how my deliverance would come. He filled me with an endless supply of grace, and He helped me carry that heavy cross up the mountain where I would be able to see the clear sky and feel the warm sun shining on my face again. The valley was deep, dark and confusing, but up on the mountain peaks I could see life from His perspective. And it was good.

After the dark, gloomy, storm-filled days, the heavy rains ceased and the angry clouds slowly began to dissipate. As the floodwaters receded, the rain was reduced to a trickle, the sky opened up, and the sun once again began to brightly shine. And lo and behold, I saw a beautiful rainbow. Its vivid colors illuminated the sky and it was a breathtaking sight. In Old Testament times, rainbows represented God's covenant promises with His people to never flood the earth again. Rainbows are my promise from God of a brighter tomorrow and a hope of a glorious future together.

That September morning I made my usual stop at the store to get my helium-filled balloons to commemorate Derrick's birthday—one mylar balloon which I would attach to the tombstone vase. The other two would once again be sent to Derrick in heaven. On my way to the cemetery, I thanked God for the nine beautiful years I had with my boy. I thanked Him for all He had done in my life since that fateful day almost twenty years ago. I am a different person today—can I be so bold as to say even better? My son did not die in vain. Jesus used this precious boy's life and death to alter the course of my destination.

As my hands let go of the two helium-filled balloons they quickly flew off into the distant sky together. A large bird was flapping its wings nearby. Then I noticed that the balloons remained attached to one another. It occurred to me that one balloon represented my son and the other balloon represented me. We were soaring off together in the sky, and then I understood that we are not separated from one another at all. Maybe in the flesh we are, but we are still very much together in spirit, and Jesus Himself is with us. God's Holy Spirit lives in my heart, and my son is in the very presence of the Lord. We are eternally connected and will be forever. He is my 'rainbow in the sky.' That is my promise from God.

My dearest Savior and Best Friend, Jesus,

How can I thank you enough? You have rescued me from the deepest, darkest pit. You have rescued me from myself. Had it not been for your unwavering love, I would have wallowed in self-pity and despair, and would have chosen to give up on life and remain in the pit. There were many times I wondered how I could go on. I felt so alone in my pain and even questioned if I was being punished for my sinfulness. I know better than that. I also know that you were with me all along. You never left me. You were crying with me, interceding for me, and beckoning me to come to you. You knew how weary I was as you felt the intensity of my pain too. But you also saw the other side of the story—one that I was not able to see yet. You knew what would become of me and you knew the purpose for which you created me for. Yes, my life story included a cross that was heavy to bear, yet with You, I would be able to carry it to glorious victory.

Though so many years have slipped by since the day you ushered Derrick into your presence, you alone know how much I still miss him. The tears still flow. I know they are precious tears to you, and one day your mighty hand will wipe away the last tear from my eyes. And you know what I envision, Jesus, when you call me home? I will see you first of all with a big smile on your face and your arms opened wide to receive me into heaven with a big bear hug. And then I will hear you whisper, "Well done, my precious child. Not one tear you have shed has been wasted. I have saved them all. See, they are all here in this bottle. Thank you for coming to me when I summoned you by name. I have a surprise for you—Look over there...he's waiting for you." And then our eyes will meet, and we will instantly recognize one another. We will run toward each other and embrace like we have never done before. All the pain and sorrow will melt away as we are finally reunited. Then something miraculous will happen. I will feel a strange sensation in my chest as my heart begins to twitch and tug. And the hole that was left in my heart on the day he died will begin to close and will be forever healed. And then he and I will hold hands and walk off alone for a little while because, you see, we have a lot of catching up to do. And you will be standing there, eyes filled with love, smiling approvingly.

Thank you, Jesus, for all you have done for me. You have truly transformed me from the inside out. You have given me the gift of hope and increased my faith exponentially. You have given me beauty for ashes and put a new song in my mouth, and I will praise you all the days of my life. I rejoice with King David as I echo his words, "You turned my wailing into dancing; you removed my sackcloth and clothed me with joy, that my heart may sing to you and not be silent. O Lord my God, I will give you thanks forever" (Psalm 30:11-12).

To You be the glory forever and ever!

Your daughter Diana, a princess of the King

Derrick's tombstone reads:
    God's Greatest Gift Returned to God –
            Our Son and Brother
            Derrick E. Cotterman
                Sept. 21, 1980
                Feb. 10, 1990

Epilogue

Though it was dusk, the beauty of the day beckoned me to linger a little while longer. It was unseasonably warm outside so I explored the sacred grounds once more. My three day retreat was coming to an end. I listened to a speaker talk about the necessity of taking breaks or 'sacred pauses' during the day to reflect on God and His goodness and grace. I spent time in solitude listening to the deep yearnings of my heart and hearing the soft, still whispers of my heavenly Father. How incredibly wonderful to hear His voice in the hidden places of my heart. His words bring such comfort, hope and healing.

I came upon a Labyrinth and decided to slowly and methodically walk through the maze as I reflected upon my life. Though my thoughts quickly reverted to the past, I chose not to linger there. Instead, my thoughts fast-forwarded toward the future. I know full well that my history is a part of my destiny. These painful experiences were not in vain. God has been with me all along, drawing me to Himself, desiring to teach and mold me into the person that would bring Him glory. I thought of my various roles—wife, mother, daughter, sister, friend. I know God is not finished with me yet. There is more living to do and more mystery to uncover.

I continued walking and soon found myself in a cemetery. It was quite large and laid out so beautifully. Little crosses represented hundreds of lives that had come and gone. This cemetery was for all the Sisters of Charity who had died during the last two hundred years since the convent was established. Once again, I reflected on the brevity of life determined to live mine to its fullest. Far off in the distance I saw a small, flickering light. I suspected it was a lit candle placed next to one of the gravesites. It seemed to call out my name as it beckoned me to come. I was intrigued so I proceeded walking toward this distant light. It must be a special gravesite for none of the others had any candles.

When I was only a few feet from the light, I realized that it was not a candle at all. It was a toy dump truck, and the light that illuminated so brightly was the toy truck's two headlights. As I looked at the foot of the tombstone I noticed many objects encircling it. Stuffed animals of various shapes and sizes, toy rattles, a Christmas stocking, and even a card placed inside a Ziploc bag were but a few of the items. My eyes fixated on the words on this special tombstone—"In memory of the little ones who rest in the palm of God's hand and for those who love them." It was donated by Good Samaritan Hospital in 1991, a year after Derrick died. Directly behind the tombstone was a huge crucifix with Jesus hanging on it. Oh, my goodness—this tombstone nestled in the far corner of a convent's cemetery was designated for all of the children who had died and gone to heaven.

Tears began to flow down my face and I felt His tears too.

I randomly picked up one of the toy teddy bears and held it close. I opened the Ziploc bag and carefully opened the envelope addressed to Matthew. It was a birthday card from his mother. I tried to read the hand-written words but was not able to for by then it was too dark. I realized that each item was lovingly placed around this tombstone by someone who loved his child very much. For the first time ever, I was so keenly aware of not only my pain, but all other parents who hurt so deeply. There are many of us, and my pain was magnified as I wept for them too. Then I looked at that little dump truck again. My thoughts returned to my own son. How Derrick loved playing with all kinds of dump trucks, garbage trucks, and construction vehicles! Was it you, Derrick, who led me here? Is this your way of letting me know that you are still with me? I was totally overwhelmed by emotion. I felt Jesus' presence. He assured me that He sees the pain that lingers and He has not forgotten. Sorrow made her appearance, but this time Joy accompanied her, and in the dark stillness of the night the four of us were there together. I welcomed them all, and I felt comfort in their presence.

Yes, I have changed. I do not know of any experience more incredibly difficult or painful than burying one's own flesh and blood. Though life goes on, those of us who have endured this suffering are not the same. Truly, a part of us died with our children. A piece of our heart remains theirs even beyond the grave, and we will not be complete or fully alive again until the day we are reunited with them. Even so, Jesus sees the other part of the story—the part we can only dream about. He anticipates the wonderful reunion that awaits us. He asks for our perseverance and trust for He knows the joy that has been set before us. It is the same joy that enabled Him to endure the cross.

Oh, Jesus, I will persevere and I will trust. This is the cross you have given me to bear. You have assigned me my cup and my portion. Though I grieve, I will not grieve as one who has no hope. I believe with full conviction that one day I will see you face to face. I envision you cradling my face in your tender hands, gently wiping away that last tear and whispering, "Well done, Diana. Now, come and see who is waiting for you." Just as the father ran toward his prodigal son to welcome him home, we'll run toward one another and embrace like never before. When our eyes meet, all the pain and sorrow will forever melt away as the hole in my heart miraculously closes. And at last I'll hear his sweet voice once again, "Welcome home, Momma."

Yet I am always with you; you hold me by my right hand. You guide me with your counsel, and afterward you will take me into glory. Whom have I in heaven but you? And earth has nothing I desire besides you. My flesh and my heart may fail, but God is the strength of my heart and my portion forever. Those who are far from you will perish; you destroy all who are unfaithful to you. But as for me, it is good to be near God. I have made the Sovereign Lord my refuge; I will tell of all your deeds.   *Psalm 73:23-28*

The small dump truck is in the lower right hand corner, below the cross.

Once I heard a song of sweetness,
As it cleft the morning air,
Sounding in its blest completeness,
Like a tender, pleading prayer;
And I sought to find the singer,
Whence the wondrous song was borne;
And I found a bird, sore wounded,
Pinioned by a cruel thorn.

I have seen a soul in sadness,
While its wings with pain were furl'd,
Giving hope, and cheer and gladness
That should bless a weeping world
And I knew that life of sweetness,
Was of pain and sorrow borne,
And a stricken soul was singing,
With its heart against a thorn.

Ye are told of One who loved you,
Of a Savior crucified,
Ye are told of nails that pinioned,
And a spear that pierced His side;
Ye are told of cruel scourging,
Of a Savior bearing scorn,
And He died for your salvation,
With His brow against a thorn.

Ye "are not above the Master."
Will you breathe a sweet refrain?
And His grace will be sufficient,
When your heart is pierced with pain.

Will you live to bless His loved ones,
Tho' your life be bruised and torn,
Like the bird that sang so sweetly,
With its heart against a thorn?

Selected

Bibliography

Cowan, Mrs. Charles E. *"Streams in the Desert."* Zondervan Publishing House: Grand Rapids, MI.1996. (Annie Johnson Flint poem and Selected poem, pg. 359).

Contact Information

If you would like to contact Diana, please send an email to: Stroh.Diana@gmail.com.

You can also follow Diana's writings at her blog site: http://diana-inthepottershands.blogspot.com